The Other
Jonathan Edwards

The Other Jonathan Edwards

Selected Writings on Society, Love, and Justice

EDITED BY

Gerald McDermott
and Ronald Story

University of Massachusetts Press
Amherst & Boston

ISBN 978-1-62534-152-5 (paperback); 151-8 (hardcover)

Designed by Jack Harrison
Set in Adobe Garamond Pro
Printed and bound by Sheridan Books

Library of Congress Cataloging-in-Publication Data

Edwards, Jonathan, 1703–1758.
[Works. Selections]
The other Jonathan Edwards : selected writings on society, love, and justice /
edited by Gerald McDermott and Ronald Story.
pages cm
Includes bibliographical references and index.
ISBN 978-1-62534-151-8 (hardcover : alk. paper) —
ISBN 978-1-62534-152-5 (pbk. : alk. paper)
1. Theology—Early works to 1800.
2. Congregational churches—Doctrines—Early works to 1800.
3. Congregational churches—United States—Sermons.
4. Reformed Church—Doctrines—History—18th century.
5. Sermons, American—18th century.
I. McDermott, Gerald R. (Gerald Robert), editor. II. Story, Ronald, editor. III. Title.
BX7260.E3A25 2015
230'.58—dc23
2015009310

British Library Cataloguing-in-Publication Data
A catalogue record for this book is available from the British Library.

To Ryan and Darrah,
who have created a beautiful little society,
and
To Peter Ives and the Congregational UCC ministry
of the Pioneer Valley

CONTENTS

ACKNOWLEDGMENTS

Gerry is grateful to his wife, Jean, for her encouragement and patience, and to Judi Pinckney for her always-cheerful help. Ron thanks Patricia Tracy and the University of Minnesota Department of Geography for permission to use material from their work in preparing the maps of Jonathan Edwards's region, and also, once again, Kerry Buckley for his keen and critical eye. Both Ron and Gerry appreciate Ken Minkema's speedy responses to our queries, and Yale University Press's permission to print these excerpts from its critical edition of the *Works of Jonathan Edwards*. The location of the selection within the critical edition is indicated on the first page of each entry.

SIGNIFICANT DATES
IN EDWARDS'S LIFE

1703   October: born at East Windsor, Connecticut

1716   September: begins undergraduate studies at Connecticut Collegiate
        School, Wethersfield (later becomes known as Yale College)

1720   May: completes baccalaureate degree
        September: delivers valedictory oration

1721   Summer: conversion experience at East Windsor

1722   May: completes graduate studies at Yale College
        August: arrives at New York City to begin preaching to English
        Presbyterian congregation

1724   Elected tutor at Yale College

1726   Chosen to be assistant to Solomon Stoddard at Northampton,
        Massachusetts, church; Edwards is given £100 salary, £300 to build a
        house, and 50 acres of land

1727   July: marries Sarah Pierpont in New Haven

1728   Daughter Sarah born

1729   Solomon Stoddard dies; Edwards becomes senior pastor at Northampton

1730   Daughter Jerusha born

1732   Daughter Esther born

1734   December: Connecticut Valley revivals begin; Edwards reports in the
        Faithful Narrative that parishioners are singing in four-part harmony,
        men taking three and women one
        Daughter Mary born

1736   Daughter Lucy born
        Fall–winter: Joseph Bellamy comes to study with Edwards

1738   April–October: preaches *Charity and Its Fruits* (published 1852)
        Son Timothy born

1739   March–August: preaches *History of the Work of Redemption* (published
        1774)

1740   Daughter Susannah born

1741   July: preaches *Sinners in the Hands of an Angry God* at Enfield,
        Connecticut (published shortly thereafter)
        August–September: "Great Awakening" peaks in Northampton
        December: Samuel Hopkins arrives to study with Edwards

1742   Edwards first introduces hymn-singing using the hymns of Isaac Watts
        Covenant renewal at Northampton
        May–end of summer: Hopkins comes back to study
        Hopkins preaches in the afternoon at Northampton "wholly without
        notes"

1743   Daughter Eunice born
        Northampton precinct votes to give public access to cut wood from and
        pasture land in the inner commons for ten more years, after which the
        lands revert to exclusive use by their owners

1745   Son Jonathan, Jr., born
        King George's War: Louisbourg taken after forty-seven-day siege

1746   June: *Religious Affections* published
        August: French and Indians take Fort Massachusetts; Edwards's
        parsonage is "forted in" and quartered with soldiers; an Indian raiding
        party attacks near Southampton

1747   *An Humble Attempt to Promote Explicit Agreement and Visible Union of
        God's People in Extraordinary Prayer* published
        Daughter Elizabeth born

1748   June: preaches funeral sermon of John Stoddard at Northampton,
        published as *A Strong Rod Broken and Withered*
        Daughter Jerusha dies

1749   December: preliminary council meets to consider controversy between
        Edwards and Northampton church

1750   Son Pierpont born
        June: dismissed as pastor of Northampton
        July: preaches *Farewell Sermon* (published 1751)
        July–November: preaches on "supply" at Northampton

1751   August: formally installed as pastor to English and Indian congregations
at Stockbridge, Massachusetts
August: Indian commissioners arrive at Stockbridge for conference
August: Mohawks arrive at Stockbridge for conference

1753   Waumpaumcorse, a Schaghticoke Indian, is murdered at Stockbridge by
two English horse thieves

1754   Summer: Edwards's parsonage is fortified and quartered with soldiers
against fears of Indian attacks
September: Schaghticokes kill four in a raid on Stockbridge
Freedom of the Will published

1755   February: completes *End for Which God Created the World*

1756   Completes bulk of *The Nature of True Virtue* (published 1765)
September: Stockbridge attacked by Indians; four English killed

1757   May: completes *Original Sin* (published 1758)
September: trustees of College of New Jersey (Princeton) write to offer
presidency

1758   February: assumes office as president of College of New Jersey;
inoculated for smallpox
March: dies of complications from inoculation
October: Sarah Pierpont Edwards dies of dysentery in Philadelphia

EUROPEAN POSSESSIONS IN AMERICA

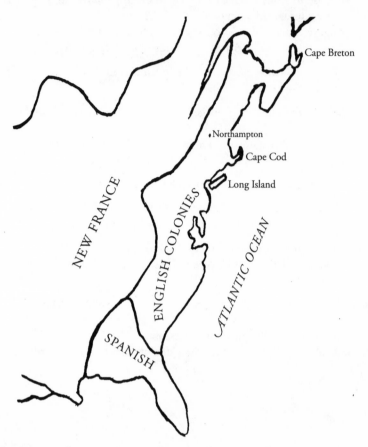

England repeatedly went to war with France from the early 1700s over European matters, and these conflicts spilled into the colonies, including North America. English colonial forces campaigned with great fierceness against the French, whose claims threatened to squeeze, or at least bottle up, the English settlements. France, unlike England, was Roman Catholic and therefore a danger to Protestantism. And because New France was sparsely settled, French soldiers fought increasingly alongside Native American allies. So at times did the English. As a result, guerrilla violence simmered all along the frontier.

The wars touched the Edwards family at many points. Timothy, Jonathan's father, was chaplain to a militia expeditionary force. Jonathan himself prayed to God to bless an assault on a French fortress at Cape Breton. Indian raids wreaked havoc on Deerfield, hard by Northampton, shortly after Jonathan's birth, and on Pittsfield, north of Stockbridge, just before his death. He once sent two of his daughters to Long Island partly to keep them safe. More than once he fortified his home, and sometimes soldiers took shelter there. England eventually destroyed French power in America, but only after Edwards's death.

ENGLISH SETTLEMENT OF NEW ENGLAND

Settlement to 1710

Settlement to 1750

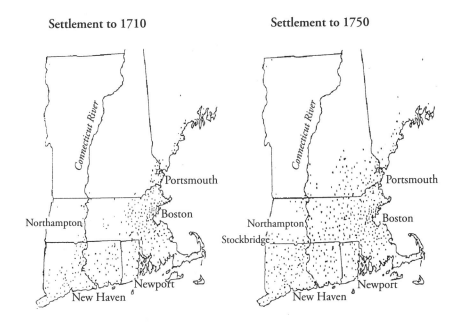

Europeans initially settled along the coast of New England where they landed and had access to Atlantic trade. Moving inland was not easy. There were no roads, only paths. Clearing the land for farming was backbreaking work, and there was much Native American resistance. As late as 1700, most settlements remained within twenty miles of the shoreline.

One exception was along the Connecticut River, which was broad and partly navigable. By the early 1700s, there were some fifty towns in the river valley. By 1750, there were many more, and others had "hived off" west, north, and east. Travel remained difficult. Edwards took two long days on horseback to reach Boston, just over one hundred miles distance. Hauling produce or driving livestock took longer. The vast northern interior, including much of far western Massachusetts, held few English and fewer French. Edwards's move to Stockbridge was a rarity.

Every new town required a new meeting house and minister, making the ministry one of the great growth professions of this era in New England. The Connecticut Valley alone had scores of pulpits to fill. The pastors who held these posts, mostly Congregationalist or Presbyterian, were usually prominent and educated enough to exert community influence—and also quarrel readily among themselves.

Source: Based in part on information drawn from Bonnie Barton, *The Comparability of Geographical Methodology* (Ann Arbor: Michigan Geographical Imprints, 1977).

NORTHAMPTON DURING EDWARDS'S MINISTRY

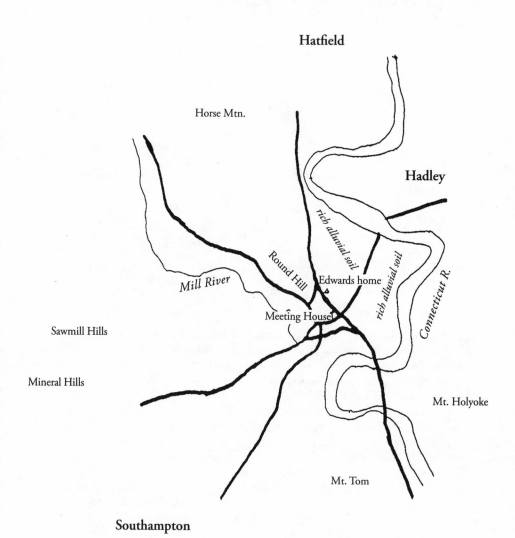

Hatfield

Horse Mtn.

Hadley

rich alluvial soil

rich alluvial soil

Edwards home

Round Hill

Mill River

Meeting House

Connecticut R.

Sawmill Hills

Mineral Hills

Mt. Holyoke

Mt. Tom

Southampton

Northampton had a population of 1,300 or 1,400 in the late 1720s, and perhaps 1,700 fifteen years later, when the Southampton section withdrew—in the standard New England way—to form its own township, thereby reducing the Northampton total. Many families lived on residential lots of around four acres each, granted free of charge by the proprietors, who also distributed arable land while it lasted. Houses were a mile or a little more from the meeting house, a manageable walking distance. The earliest settlers farmed the best land, to the east along the river, which they bequeathed to their heirs. Pasture and wood lots, crucial for heat, ran back into hilly, less productive terrain. Tradesmen—skilled carpenters, blacksmiths—frequently flourished, as did well-situated farmers, who added acreage over the years.

Farming was mostly subsistence: gardens, apple orchards, livestock, timber, and grain. Clothing and furniture, like beer and cider, were, with rare exceptions, made locally. The town paid Edwards well for a small country community and threw a parsonage and new barn into the bargain. But inflation sapped his salary, which had to support many children and also guests drawn by Edwards's renown. The Edwardses raised sheep, sometimes driving them overland to Boston for extra income. The family's removal to Stockbridge in the 1750s meant, for a time, real hardship.

Source: Based in part on information drawn from Patricia Tracy, *Jonathan Edwards, Pastor* (New York: Hill and Wang, 1980).

First Meeting House, 1655–1661

The first large structure of any kind erected in the new settlement, this building was typical of the New England frontier: rough-hewn exterior, a few small windows, seating for a few dozen people.

Second Meeting House, 1661–1737

The second meeting house, where Edwards's grandfather Solomon Stoddard preached for many decades, was in Puritan style: plain door frame, no overhang, four-square windows, wide plank sheathing. The building might accommodate several hundred people for town or church affairs. There was no stove. A system of assigned pews with closeable half doors was intended partly to acknowledge status and partly for warmth.

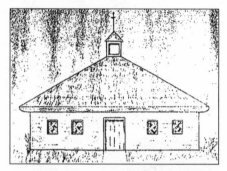

Third Meeting House, 1737–1812

Built during Edwards's ministry, the third meeting house seated some eight hundred people, many of them brought into church membership during the Valley Revival of the mid-1730s. The building's exterior—two stories, double window rows, entryway with high bell tower, soaring steeple—reflected the town's increased wealth and possibly its minister's fame. There was still no heat, as in other New England churches, but much squabbling over family pew rights, which dismayed Edwards. Some people in the pews now faced away from the pulpit, which further upset him.

Meeting house depictions courtesy of Historic Northampton, First Churches of Northampton, and Marcia Kennick.

The Other
Jonathan Edwards

INTRODUCTION

Most Americans know Jonathan Edwards (1703–1758)—if they know him at all—as the preacher of "Sinners in the Hands of an Angry God." Many conclude that he is not only intimidating but repulsive, because of the wrathful God he depicts in painful detail. Few know that Edwards was actually obsessed not just by God's wrath but by God's beauty, as many scholars have shown over the last half century in what has become a renaissance of interest in Edwards across many disciplines.

But even those who know that Edwards was far more than a hellfire and damnation preacher—in fact, he was one of the greatest theologians North America has ever produced (Yale University Press recently completed publication of a seventy-three-volume critical edition of his works)—typically have no idea of the range of his interests. Most think he was only concerned about getting people out of hell and into heaven, and thought little about the world outside the church. The fact of the matter is that Edwards paid great attention to what we call the secular world, and developed a theology of society that was more sophisticated than that of his published peers in Boston.

Nor do most people know that in the many writings that contribute to that public theology, Edwards had plenty to say about themes that are as relevant today as ever—love, justice, and society. This reader gives you a glimpse of what is a far larger body of writings on these subjects. But first, a look at Edwards's social context.

Edwards's Social World

The prevailing social ideal of prerevolutionary America was that of the deferential society. This view of society was founded on both political theory and philosophy. Political theorists such as James Harrington and John Locke argued that government originated from the mutual consent of members of a society that had organized for the purpose of protecting property. Those with more property naturally deserved more representation in the governance of society.

The philosophical basis for the deferential society was what was called the "Great Chain of Being."[1] This was the idea that reality consists of an ascending ladder of beings, from the tiniest amoeba, to plants, animals, humans, angels, and, finally, God. It was thought that this laddered structure of existence, with all of its rungs, was perfect and therefore the best of all possible worlds. Applied to human society, this metaphysics (a philosophy of what underlies all existence) legitimated the status quo. Goodness and beauty were identified not with material and social plenty for all but with fullness and diversity in the social order. Every level of society, including that of the abjectly poor, was necessary for the fullest manifestation of beauty. So inequality and even evil were necessary to make perfect the rest of existence.[2]

Therefore, a hierarchical society was ordered in the way that is best for the cosmos, and it made sense that the educated, propertied elite were in control. God had fitted them for their positions, which implied that they possessed the wisdom they needed for their roles.

The lower classes of colonial America seem to have agreed with this assessment, since they regularly elected their "betters" to public office. Many pastors, influenced by Puritan theologians, instructed social "inferiors" to demonstrate respect by standing when their social superiors rode by, offering them the best seats, allowing them to speak first, addressing them by their titles, and obeying them because "every higher power is the ordinance of God" (Romans 13:1).

The selections included here show that although Edwards was a hierarchicalist of sorts—writing that "heads, princes or governors" deserve honor and obedience—he did not elaborate on the gradations among humans as other parsons did, but instead criticized existing ideas of who

1. Arthur O. Lovejoy, *The Great Chain of Being: A Study of the History of an Idea* (Cambridge: Harvard University Press, 1964).

2. The German philosopher Gottfried Wilhelm Leibniz provided the classic defense of the idea that evil is necessary for this, the best of all possible worlds, in his *Theodicy*, ed. Austin Farrer, trans. E. M. Huggard (1710; New Haven: Yale University Press, 1952).

is great and who is not. While some of his contemporaries said the poor were poor because of their laziness or because God had put them there, Edwards pleaded on behalf of the marginalized and exposed the moral corruption of some of the elite:

> There are many great men of the world, noble men and kings and men of great power and policy, men of noble blood and honorable descent, men of great wealth, men of vast learning and knowledge in the world, that are greatly honored and make a great figure, and great account is made of 'em in the world, that are wicked men and reprobates; and they all ben't of so great value in God's sight as one poor saint.[3]

On the other hand, Edwards did not conceive of social equality in the way that people of the twenty-first century do. He shared some of his culture's prejudices about African Americans and slavery. He and his wife, Sarah, owned at least one slave, and he believed that the Bible allowed slavery. In some respects, however, Edwards distanced himself from the racism so prevalent in his day. He said that blacks and Indians were not inherently inferior ("we are made of the same human race"), and that in the future "many of the Negroes and Indians will be divines." Blacks and Indians were spiritual equals to whites, he preached. His Northampton, Massachusetts, church admitted nine Africans to full membership during his years there. Edwards worked consistently and courageously to defend Indians against whites (including his own relatives) who wanted to steal their lands. In his defense of the institution of slavery, Edwards nonetheless condemned the African slave trade, saying no nations "have any power or business to disenfranchise all the nations of Africa." His own son Jonathan, Jr., and his foremost disciple, Samuel Hopkins, were early, outspoken abolitionists, and Hopkins's abolitionism was inspired by his reading of Edwards's treatise *The Nature of True Virtue*.

Edwards was also somewhat progressive in that era in his attitudes toward women. Puritans did not generally believe it was important to educate girls, and "female learning" was ridiculed even in the revolu-

---

3. Edwards, "Christians a Chosen Generation," in *The Works of Jonathan Edwards*, vol. 17, *Sermons and Discourses, 1730–1733*, ed. Mark Valeri (New Haven: Yale University Press, 1999), 311. Longer quotations are cited in this introduction but shorter ones are not. All of the latter are taken from the Yale edition of the *Works*, the volumes of which are listed in the "For Further Reading" section at the back of this reader.

tionary period. In contrast, Edwards urged that Indian girls be given the same educational privileges as boys. Women's testimony in religious meetings was typically condemned in Edwards's day, but he encouraged the practice of female testifying during the religious revivals in the 1730s and 1740s. When other religious leaders wrote that women were more inclined than men to religious delusion, Edwards used women—and not a single man!—as personal illustrations of true religion in his two major accounts of these revivals. He likewise hinted that women are more spiritually sensitive than men. These beliefs, made public in his sermons and writings, could explain why women generally supported him when he was thrown out of his pulpit by a majority of the men in Northampton.

This era also included a bias against young people. A man in western Massachusetts without land and wife was considered less than a full and independent member of society—even though it was nearly impossible to get married without land, and land came only by inheritance or purchase at very high prices. Edwards made a special appeal to young men to gain conversion and thus become full members—an unconventional appeal in his time. He made similar entreaties to servants and slaves, welcoming those who converted to full membership in the church: "Hearken to the call of Christ . . . young men and maids, old men, middle aged and little children, both male and female, both black and white, high and low, rich and poor together."[4] Servants and slaves who were regarded as "low" could think of themselves as spiritually equal to their masters and others who considered themselves "high."

Edwards's Economic World

Edwards spent most of his adult years as pastor in Northampton, one of the largest towns in the Connecticut River Valley. Its thriving economy was based on agriculture and trade. As it prospered in the 1730s and after, its elite engaged in what we might call conspicuous consumption—showing others how important they were by purchasing luxury items. As the economy expanded in the next decade and a half, familiar economic

4. Sermon on Matthew 22:9–10, quoted in Perry Miller, "Jonathan Edwards's Sociology of the Great Awakening," *New England Quarterly* 21 (March–December 1948): 72, 77.

problems emerged including inflation, depreciated currency, trade imbalances, government deficits, poor investments, and indebtedness for many. The gap between rich and poor widened.

This gap had been spreading since the end of the seventeenth century. Not only were there the usual disparities in income, but the psychological distance between upper and lower classes also seemed to be getting bigger. In 1692, when it was proposed (and passed) that the education of all Northampton children be paid out of a common fund, some wealthy citizens objected.

A similar change occurred in the town's handling of a poorhouse. It had been the custom in seventeenth-century Northampton to use town funds or private charity to board the poor in wealthier homes. In 1705, the town voted to build a poorhouse. For unexplained reasons, it was never built but there was also no return to seventeenth-century practice. The same pattern can be seen in the town's road maintenance. Before 1700, all able-bodied men were required to put in time working on the roads. By Edwards's time, the town had hired a constable and permanent road workers, and paid for them out of town monies. In 1715, the town ratified preexisting land allotments without mentioning public rights to wood on common fields. Access by the less advantaged to sources for firewood became a common cause for dispute in later years. As time went on, these contentions revealed increasing divisions among economic classes.

Edwards's responses to these economic disparities were noticeably different from those of leading lights in Boston. One famous preacher, Jonathan Mayhew, described the hunger pains of the impoverished as "the natural effects of intemperance and other vices," and God's way "to chastise and thereby to reform" them.[5] Edwards instead exhorted his hearers to do whatever they could to relieve the needs of the poor, even if the poor were already receiving welfare from public funds (see no. 6, "The State of Public Affairs"). In the 1740s, he made it the "principal business" of the Northampton deacons to take care of the poor, and called on his wealthier parishioners to make frequent contributions to the church fund for the poor. In contrast, Charles Chauncy, another

---

5. Jonathan Mayhew, *Two Sermons on the Nature, Extent and Perfection of the Divine Goodness* (Boston: D. & J. Kneeland, 1763), 61–62.

leading Boston pastor, did not set up such a deacon's fund until the 1770s.

Edwards's Religious World

Edwards was raised at the tail end of the Puritan tradition. The Puritans might be described as the marching wing of the Church of England. They had rejected the fixed forms and practices of traditional Catholicism in favor of a freer, less structured form of faith and worship, and a set of beliefs and practices that they believed were based on the Bible rather than human traditions. In their zeal to glorify God, they used severe discipline within their communities to enforce strict conformity to all of God's "ordinances," such as regular church attendance and observance of the sacraments. Speaking broadly, there was a twofold focus in Puritanism—an inward stress on the cultivation of a God-pleasing spiritual life, and an outward stress on the reform of church structures and more broadly of society itself to conform to God's purposes. Puritans viewed themselves as a "chosen people," like the ancient Israelites. They sought to achieve in New England something that they believed had not been accomplished in the rest of Christendom since the time of the Protestant Reformation—reliving the ideals of the early New Testament church without the encumbrances of Catholicism.

Most New England Puritans called themselves "Congregationalists" because they defined the church solely in terms of local congregations bound by strict agreements ("covenants"), and therefore they refused to recognize any binding authority outside of these congregations, such as councils, bishops, archbishops, or popes. Congregationalists thought the Anglicans had erred in founding churches not on the basis of common belief and confession but on geographical location (that is, the local parish church) under the control of bishops—whose offices Puritans considered unbiblical.

The New Englanders' stress on churches composed of "visible saints" raised many questions as to how, when, and where each person was to demonstrate a genuine profession of faith, and who exactly was to make this determination. During the 1630s, churches in New England began to require members to give not merely generalized professions of faith but specific recountings (known as a "relation") regarding their own personal experiences of God's work in their souls. Only full adult members who had made this relation had the right to commune at the Lord's Supper and bring their children for baptism. But when many of the next generation failed to be able to give relations, New England's leaders devised the Half-Way Covenant (1662), which extended infant baptism so that it was available not only to the children of parents who were baptized and *professing* but also the children of parents who were baptized yet *unprofessing*.

This decision made baptism a kind of hereditary birthright in families with early New England roots. Despite controversy, most congregations eventually made their peace with the "half-way" approach, which required a double-booking system for full members and half-members. Further controversy erupted after the publication of Solomon Stoddard's *The Doctrine of Instituted Churches Explained* (1700), which affirmed the notion of national churches, denied the necessity of church covenants, and allowed the admission of unconverted persons to the Lord's Supper. For Stoddard, who was Edwards's grandfather, the Lord's Supper could function as a "converting ordinance." These early debates over church membership and admission to the sacraments were part of the background to the later communion controversy in Northampton and to Edwards's eventual dismissal from his pastorate there in 1750. It is noteworthy that Edwards's father, Timothy Edwards, contended with his congregation during the 1730s over his stringency regarding admission to baptism and the Lord's Supper.

Religious opinions during the 1700s were not restricted to debates over church membership and admission to the Lord's Supper. Instead there was a spectrum of views. On one extreme were deists, who denied the deity of Christ, the need for atonement on the cross, and the Trinity. The deists reflected a broad tendency toward a moralizing or ethicizing of Christianity. Many intellectuals presumed that religion existed to promote good behavior. Anthony Ashley-Cooper, Third Earl of Shaftesbury, wrote that "the end of religion is to make us more perfect and more accomplished in all our duties and moral obligations." Benjamin Franklin, who was born the same year as Edwards, commented that the problem with doctrinal sermons is that they made their hearers good Presbyterians rather than good citizens. Some deists held that Christian teachings had value in enforcing morality, even if the teachings, taken literally, were false. When the deist writer Anthony Collins was asked why he sent his household servants to church when he did not attend himself, he replied, "I do it that they may neither rob nor murder me."[6]

Closer to the views of Calvinists like Edwards was the position known as Arminianism, named after the Dutch theologian Arminius. Arminians believed in the atonement, Trinity, and Christ's deity—all of which deists denied. But unlike Calvinists, they held that Christ died for all humanity (rather than just for the elect), that divine predestination hinges on God's foreknowledge of human faith or obedience (rather than simply God's loving choice), that human beings have free will to accept Christ and salvation (Calvinists said the will to accept was a gift of God), and that it is possible for those once saved to fall away permanently and thus lose their eternal salvation (Calvinists taught that true regeneration was permanent).

It was the development of Arminian views among the New England clergy and deist writings in England during the 1730s through the 1750s that provoked some of Edwards's weightiest writings, such as *Freedom of the Will, Original Sin, End of Creation,* and *Nature of True Virtue.* In the course of his reflection, writing, and publication, Edwards engaged a large number of authors—both within and outside of conventional Christian tradition. His purpose was to draw on what he thought to be the best of the Enlightenment to reformulate Christian faith in ways that could be comprehended by the educated and yet remain faithful to the basic teachings of historic faith. For example, he agreed with the Enlightenment that God acts according to the "natural fitness of things." He also tried to show that the Christian doctrine of original sin is not unjust, which was in accord with the Enlightenment insistence that God must be fair. Furthermore, Edwards labored throughout his life to demonstrate what he called "the sweet harmony between Christianity and

6. Anthony Ashley Cooper, Third Earl of Shaftesbury, *Characteristics of Men, Manners, Opinions, Times,* (1737) ed. Lawrence E. Klein (Cambridge: Cambridge University Press, 1999), 196; Benjamin Franklin, *Autobiography and Selections from Other Writings* (New Haven: Yale University Press, 1964), 147; Anthony Collins, quoted in Mark Pattison, "Tendencies of Religious Thought in England, 1688–1750," in *Essays and Reviews,* ed. John William Parker (London: Longman, Green, 1861), 274.

7. For more on Edwards and the Enlightenment, see Gerald McDermott, *Jonathan Edwards Confronts the Gods: Christian Theology, Enlightenment Religion, and Non-Christian Faiths* (New York: Oxford University Press, 2000), 218–27.

reason." This was not precisely how most Enlightenment thinkers put it, but it agreed with their sense that God and the world operate in ways that reason can discern.[7]

Edwards's Life and Work

The fifth of eleven children and the only boy, Edwards was born on October 5, 1703, into a ministerial family in East Windsor, Connecticut. His father, the Reverend Timothy Edwards, had earned the terminal theological degree (M.A.) from Harvard, and over his sixty years of ministry was known as one of Connecticut's most learned pastors. Esther Stoddard Edwards, Jonathan's mother, directed women in the Bible and theology. Her father, the Reverend Solomon Stoddard, was the famous "Pope" of the Connecticut River Valley, a theologian in his own right and powerful preacher.

Timothy and Esther homeschooled (as most educated parents did) their only son in the Bible, Reformed theology, the Greco-Roman classics, and ancient languages. They started him in Latin at age six; by the age of twelve he was reading Latin, Greek, and a smattering of Hebrew. He started college (the Connecticut Collegiate School, which later became Yale) at one month shy of his thirteenth birthday, the usual age, and graduated in 1720 at age sixteen after studying grammar, rhetoric, logic, ancient history, arithmetic, geometry, astronomy, metaphysics, ethics, and natural science. This was supplemented by theological studies in the works of the sixteenth-century French Reformer John Calvin and other theologians influenced by him.

After graduating as valedictorian of his class, Edwards proceeded to two years of graduate study at Yale. It was during this period, in his seventeenth year, that he experienced what seems to have been his conversion. In his *Personal Narrative,* written perhaps twenty years later, Edwards recalled that while he had built a prayer booth in a swamp as a child and often felt "much affected," it was only in the spring of 1721, while meditating on I Timothy 1:17, that he came to see the beauty of God's holiness, and no longer felt God's sovereignty (ultimate control of all things) was a "horrible" doctrine.

After completing graduate studies, Edwards preached at an English Presbyterian congregation in New York City for eight months (August

1722–April 1723). New York City then had about seven thousand inhabitants, and Edwards's little church was near what we now call Ground Zero, toward the bottom of Manhattan Island. Here he started his spiritual "Diary" and "Resolutions," whose ardent yearnings still excite young readers but weary their seniors. For example, Edwards wrote, "Resolved, never to do any manner of thing, whether in soul or body, less or more, but what tends to the glory of God; nor be, nor suffer it, if I can avoid it. . . . Resolved, to strive to my utmost every week to be brought higher in religion, and to a higher exercise of grace, than I was the week before."

It was in this New York pastorate that Edwards also started his *Miscellanies,* theological notebooks that eventually grew to more than one million words. Here Edwards began his emphasis on beauty that evolved into the most developed aesthetic theology in the history of western Christian thought. His very first entry in these massive notebooks, at about age twenty, proposed, "Holiness is a most beautiful and lovely thing. . . . 'Tis the highest beauty and amiableness, vastly above all other beauties." Edwards continued here and in his published works to argue that "God is God, and distinguished from all other beings, and exalted above 'em, chiefly by his divine beauty, which is infinitely diverse from all other beauty." He went on to develop his conviction that God's nature is the essence of beauty, the criterion of all beauty, and the source or fountain for all beauty in the world.

After a brief tenure as pastor in Bolton, Connecticut, Edwards accepted Yale's invitation to be its senior tutor—in effect, president—in May 1724, and spent the next two years there. This was a difficult time for the young professor because of unruly students and frequent sickness. His diary and letters reveal that saintliness did not come easily. He was sometimes "violently beset with temptation," and would figure "some sum in Arithmetic or Geometry" for relief. During this time and throughout his life, there were periods of depression interspersed with occasional experiences of spiritual ecstasy. By the end of his Yale tenure, he was world-weary: he felt "fears, perplexities, multitudes of cares and distraction of mind." He seemed glad to accept his grandfather Stoddard's invitation in 1726 to come to Northampton as junior pastor.

Edwards was twenty-three when he arrived, and spent the next twenty-three years in what was the largest and most influential New England church outside of Boston, preaching two sermons every Sabbath in an academic gown and powdered periwig (as was the custom then), and delivering a lecture on most Wednesdays. In 1729, two years after Edwards had been ordained at Northampton, Stoddard died and Edwards took over as senior pastor.

Less than a year after arriving at Northampton, Edwards married Sarah Pierpont, whose minister father was a founder of Yale. Some years before, Jonathan had been smitten by Sarah's "wonderful sweetness, calmness and universal benevolence of mind." Their marriage, which evangelist George Whitefield thought "sweeter" than any he had seen, produced eleven children.

Three of his most famous addresses in the 1730s sounded recurring themes in his theology. The first was a lecture invited in 1731 by the Boston clergy. This was a prestigious opportunity that was also intimidating, since Edwards did not share the Harvard credentials of the town's leading clergy. Edwards challenged Arminian presumptions with his *God Glorified in the Work of Redemption by the Greatness of Man's Dependence on Him,* which became his first published book. Edwards emphasized two themes that were developed through the rest of his career—God's sovereignty and the Trinity.

In *A Divine and Supernatural Light* (1734), Edwards outlined the source and nature of true religion. He argued that it does not come from natural convictions such as conscience or mere impressions on the imagination, but is instead a taste or vision of the beauty of God in Christ. God uses means such as scripture and preaching to convey this sense, but the true cause is the immediate work of the Holy Spirit.

Later that same year, Edwards revisited the theme of his Masters *Questio* for a lecture that became his first published treatise, *Justification by Faith Alone.* His main purpose was to teach that people should not "trust in their own righteousness for justification, which is a thing fatal to the soul." But Edwards went further than Reformation platitudes when he warned that "a man is not justified by faith only, but also by works," when works are understood as the proper "acts or expressions of faith."

This lecture on justification, which Edwards turned into two sermons, made a deep impression on the Northampton congregation, especially its young people. Before too long, the Connecticut Valley Revival broke out, eventually culminating in a spiritual earthquake that rocked not only Edwards's own congregation but spread to towns up and down the Connecticut River. Unlike previous revivals under Stoddard and other Puritans, this awakening reached as many men as women and many older people. Within three months, three hundred (half the adults) in Edwards's church said they were converted. Most of the rest were seeking or moved. The whole town, Edwards reported in his *Faithful Narrative* (1738), "seemed to be full of the presence of God; it never was so full of love, nor so full of joy." Church services were packed, often marked by tears of sorrow for sin and the unconverted, and tears of joy and love.

In 1739, Edwards moved in his preaching and writing to a survey of the vast *History of Redemption,* from before the creation to after the millennium (a thousand-year period where Christ would rule the earth) at the end of the world. In a series of thirty sermons, Edwards chronicled in both sacred and secular history the coordination of history and scripture, attempting to show how the sacred and secular interpenetrate under God's direction, and also how history is a massive demonstration of the truths of Reformed theology.

A year after he delivered his *History of Redemption* series, the dam burst. Historians have referred to the resulting flood as the Great Awakening. The downpours of the spirit were triggered by Whitefield's preaching tour of the colonies in 1739, and fed by Edwards's famous sermon, "Sinners in the Hands of an Angry God."

In the next decade, Edwards rose to become the foremost theologian of awakening and revival, writing *Distinguishing Marks of a Work of the Spirit of God* (1741) and *Some Thoughts Concerning the Revival* (1742) to defend the revivals.

But after this awakening subsided, and as many of its converts returned to worldly ways, Edwards became more circumspect about judging whether religious experience produces regeneration (spiritual rebirth). His *Religious Affections* (1746) is a careful exploration of the nature of true religion, and good and bad ways of discerning its presence. The book argues, first, that religious experience is centered in what he called the "affections." By this Edwards meant strong inclinations of the soul that are manifested in thinking, feeling, and choosing. The affections are not emotions but give rise to emotion; they are strong inclinations and not simply preferences; and they involve mind, will, and feeling at the same time. People with true religious affections will focus more on God than themselves. The regenerate person will be grateful for what God has done in Christ for her, but her principal motivation for Christian life will be the beauty of the holiness she sees in Jesus Christ. Seeing that beauty is the very center of Edwards's vision of God:

> This is the beauty of the Godhead, and the divinity of Divinity (if I may so speak), the good of the infinite Fountain of Good; without which God himself (if that were possible to be) would be an infinite evil: without which, we ourselves had better never have been; and without which there had better have been no being. He therefore in effect knows nothing, that knows not this: his knowledge is but the shadow of knowledge, or the form of knowledge, as the Apostle [Paul] calls it.[8]

"Christian practice" (behavior) is Edwards's twelfth and most important sign of regeneration, "the chief of all the signs of grace, both as an evidence of the sincerity of professors unto others, and also to their own consciences." This does not mean perfection but commitment over time to the lordship of Christ. What someone does in her life is finally more illustrative of grace than what she says.

If the 1740s was a decade in which Edwards developed a sophisticated theology of awakening and spiritual discernment, it also saw the culmination of his lifelong passion for eschatology (last things). When he wrote his spiritual autobiography, the *Personal Narrative,* in his thirties, he recalled being dazzled by the millennial future in his twentieth year: "Sometimes Mr. Smith [a friend] and I walked there [in New York] together, to converse of the things of God; and our conversation used much to turn on the advancement of Christ's kingdom in the world, and the glorious things that God would accomplish for his church in the latter days."

In that same year, Edwards published *An Humble Attempt to Promote Explicit Agreement and Visible Union of God's People in Extraordinary Prayer for the Revival of Religion and the Advancement of Christ's Kingdom on Earth.* Its purpose was to bring about "that *last* and greatest enlargement and most glorious advancement of the church of God on earth"—a long period of revival that would eventuate in a literal millennium—by means of a "concert of prayer" in which churches in the

---

8. Edwards, *The Works of Jonathan Edwards,* vol. 2, *Religious Affections,* ed. John E. Smith (New Haven: Yale University Press, 1959), 274.

British Isles and the colonies would meet monthly to pray for this end-time "abundant effusion of his Holy Spirit on all the churches."

In 1750, New England was shocked when an overwhelming major-ity of voting members of the Northampton church—all male—moved to dismiss Edwards from the pastorate. Tensions had been rising since 1744, when Edwards called out publicly several young, single men in the church for harassing single women with knowledge gained from a midwife's illustrated manual, that day's version of pornography. Others were offended by his beliefs, expressed in *Religious Affections,* that quali-fications for full church membership should be tightened—beliefs that he made explicit in 1748 and 1749. When Edwards formally proposed in 1749 to change qualifications for communion—thus rejecting Stod-dard's open communion policy—by restricting it to those who could tell him they hoped they were regenerate by pointing to signs of grace in their lives, Edwards faced open revolt. Many felt their own status as members was threatened, as well as their chances of having their chil-dren baptized.

There were other factors. Edwards had contended with the congrega-tion for years over his salary, and his attempts to rewrite a church cov-enant (see no. 14, "A Church Covenant") with new behavioral standards persuaded many that his criteria were what biographer George Marsden has called "virtually monastic."[9] Edwards's refusal to make regular house calls, and his repeated sermonic chidings of parishioners' beliefs and be-havior over the years, especially those of the movers and shakers in town, contributed to the growing resentment. After preaching a sobering and plaintive farewell sermon that reminded his listeners they would all meet again before God, Edwards and his family endured a humiliating year of preaching to these same people in order to pay his bills. Finally, in the summer of 1751, Edwards moved into exile as a missionary to a small English congregation and 150 Mahican and Mohawk families in Stock-bridge in far western Massachusetts.

The Stockbridge years (August 1751–January 1758) were no retreat from conflict. The village was crowded with refugees (from the colo-nial wars with the French and their Indian allies) and soldiers, some of

9. George M. Marsden, *Jonathan Edwards: A Life* (New Haven: Yale University Press, 2003), 160.

whom took shelter in the Edwardses' home. One Sunday morning in 1754 between services, Canadian Indians ("doubtless instigated by the French," Edwards charged) attacked and killed four white worshipers. The mission was wracked by recurrent party strife between Edwards and the same Williams clan (his own cousins) that had helped to drive him out of Northampton.

But troubles within and without did not prevent Edwards from applying himself assiduously to his missionary tasks. For the seven years until he departed for Princeton, New Jersey, in January 1758, Edwards held four services most Sundays: two for his Indian charges and two for the white congregation. During the week, while working on his scholarly projects, he worked hard to defend his Indians against the depredations of whites trying to steal their lands and privileges. He wrote letters on their behalf, both to Boston and to London, procured land and had it plowed for them, and secured homes for Indian boys so that they could go to school. He even lodged one of the boys in his own home.

In the midst of this turmoil, Edwards wrote four of his greatest works. *Freedom of the Will* (1754), his most important treatise in philosophical theology, took up the question of how to reconcile divine sovereignty with human freedom. At Stockbridge Edwards also labored to respond to the Enlightenment view of human nature, which John Taylor's *Scripture-Doctrine of Original Sin* (1740) had recently unfolded. Taylor wrote that human nature is essentially good, that it is not nature but free will that leads to human corruption, and that the imputation of Adam's sin to us is unjust. In his own *Original Sin* (1758), Edwards pointed to the universality of sin and evil throughout history to challenge Taylor's first contention.

Edwards's last two treatises, *The End for Which God Created the World* and *Nature of True Virtue* (published in tandem in 1765), were meant to be read together. Both were responses to deist attacks on the God of orthodoxy as an egotistical being obsessed with applause. Edwards replied that God knows that he is infinitely the most valuable being, so it is fitting that other beings should recognize this with praise, because it conforms to the "true nature and proportion of things." It is also the case, according to Edwards, that humans' greatest happiness comes from devoting their lives to God and his praise. Therefore, God's glory and human flourishing are one and the same.

True Virtue's first chapter singles out "the more considerable Deists" as the ultimate proof of universal agreement among religious thinkers "that virtue most essentially consists in love." This treatise is fundamentally an attack on "schemes of religion or philosophy" that are concerned with ethics but "have not a supreme regard to God, and love to him." In all such schemes, Edwards pronounced peremptorily, "there is nothing of the nature of true virtue or religion in them." In other words, *True Virtue* argues that ethics without religion is something of a castle resting on air, for without a foundation in the ultimate nature of things, talk of moral duties is arbitrary. In contrast, true virtue is "consent and union with being in general." This alone is "the primary and most essential beauty."

At the end of 1757, the trustees of the College of New Jersey at Princeton invited Edwards to become the school's new president. When he wrote to accept their offer, he said he was planning to write his full version of the *History of the Work of Redemption,* a *Harmony of the Old and New Testament* (which would include messianic prophecies, symbols in the Old Testament pointing to the New, and the doctrinal harmony between the Testaments), and "many other things." At the beginning of 1758, he moved to Princeton and assumed office on February 16. Shortly thereafter, however, smallpox broke out in a nearby town, the college trustees recommended inoculations, and Edwards set an example by getting inoculated on February 23. Tragically, the serum was corrupted, and Edwards's throat became so swollen that he could not swallow the medicine he needed. On his deathbed, he asked his physician to tell his wife that their "uncommon union . . . has been of such a nature, as I trust is spiritual, and therefore will continue forever." He instructed that "as to my funeral . . . any additional sum of money that might be expected to be laid out that way, I would have it disposed of to charitable uses." Edwards died on March 22, 1758.

Edwards's Social Vision

Edwards was convinced that religion cannot be understood apart from its social manifestations. True religion, he preached and wrote, necessarily has social expression. It is concerned for the good of others and the world. Religion without social concern is therefore false. But mere social concern by itself is not true religion. For true religious affections come from a transformed heart, pervaded by the spirit of God, who moves the believer to works of love.

Historians have long known that Edwards was passionate about religious experience. This passion is what lent a special power to his sermons and treatises. It is also what moved the awakenings of the 1730s and 1740s, most of which he led and defended (though he did not defend awakeners who focused more on the self than God). But what many historians of Edwards and American religion have not known is that for Edwards, religious sensibility was never to be divorced from its social expression. Inner spiritual experience and outward social action were movements of the same soul with true affections, pieces of the same cloth.

For Edwards, the good society is one that is animated by love. This is a love that springs from a heart that sees the beauty of the Godhead. Therefore, the social duties urged by New England politicians who did not also support spiritual transformation might have improved living conditions but were incapable of producing a beautiful society. Only the religious experience that is centered in apprehension of God's beauty in Christ and his redemption could be a basis for effective social transformation. This does not mean that Edwards criticized social improvements created by the unconverted. He encouraged the converted to cooperate with the unconverted for the sake of common moral objectives, but insisted that those achievements would fall short of optimal benefit without the spiritual renovation of all involved.

Edwards regularly criticized self-centeredness and individualism. He said they were based on the illusion that we have no final relation to one another. The truth, he taught, is the opposite. All human beings "have all the same nature, like faculties, like dispositions, like desires of good, like needs, like aversion to misery, and are made of one blood." Therefore, the person who lived a self-centered life came under his withering scorn: "He that is all for himself and none for his neighbors deserves to be cut off from the benefit of human society, and to be turned out among wild beasts, to subsist as well as he can. A private niggardly spirit is more suitable for wolves and other beasts of prey, than for human beings."[10]

---

10. These quotations are from Edwards's sermon "The Duty of Charity to the Poor," in Valeri, ed., *Sermons and Discourses*, 376.

At the center of Edwards's social vision was his idea of Christian love. This was a fundamental reaching beyond the self to the other. It was a reorientation of concern from self to neighbor—"contrary to a self-ish spirit." In *Charity and Its Fruits,* a series of sermons on the Bible's love chapter (I Corinthians 13), Edwards asserted that "they who have a Christian spirit seek not only their own things but also the things of others." The ideal human being is one who gets involved in the lives of others to help them and the community: Love "disposes persons to be public spirited. A man of a right spirit is not of a narrow, private spirit; but he is greatly concerned for the good of the public community to which he belongs, and particularly of the town where he dwells."[11]

Edwards was not afraid to challenge selfishness and greed from the pulpit. In his sermon at Colonel John Stoddard's funeral (no. 17, "A Strong Rod Broken and Withered"), he criticized businessmen who took advantage of market conditions to gain exorbitant profits from the poor. When the church elders gave the best seats in the new church building to the wealthy, he denounced them in a sermon. His 1742 covenant (no. 14, "A Church Covenant") requiring Northampton entrepreneurs not to cheat in business dealings was not appreciated by town merchants and probably created resentments that contributed to his ejection in 1750.

Readers of the selections that follow will see that Edwards did not merely draw pictures of visionary communities in the sky but used his pulpit and study to subject eighteenth-century political leaders to heav-enly ideals. He did this in a number of ways. First, he shifted the place of authority from the social hierarchy to the inner recesses of the heart. By this move, he exposed the spiritual poverty of many of New England's movers and shakers, and proclaimed the spiritual authority of some of the region's poorest but God-fearing citizens. Edwards never preached social revolution, but his ennoblement of the common believer may have given confidence to some colonials to challenge society's elites.

Second, Edwards resisted many cultural norms by teaching that God is found in the poor, and that God often calls the undistinguished into his kingdom more frequently than he calls the famous and well-to-do.

---

11. All of the quotations in this paragraph are from the sermon "Charity Contrary to a Selfish Spirit," in *The Works of Jonathan Edwards,* vol. 8, *Ethical Writings,* ed. Paul Ramsey (New Haven: Yale University Press, 1989), 259, 260.

He insisted that Christians serve God by serving the underprivileged, and called on both church and state to assist the poor.

Third, Edwards went after the wealthy who had closed their hearts to the needs of those on the bottom of society. He preached that some profits were excessive, and criticized merchants who took undue advantage of people who had reached points of desperation. He warned that God would defend the poor, sometimes in astonishing ways, such as striking dead those who did not contribute to the town's programs for the poor.

In sum, Edwards did not hide in the ivory tower of his study or pulpit, shielded from the social and economic problems of his day. He fought for the disadvantaged, both whites and Indians, and probed the inequities in society at large and within his own church. He was not afraid of offending the elite of colonial New England. This determination to tell it like it is might explain why Edwards spent most of his last decade banished to the frontier.

READING
SELECTIONS

1

Sermon: "Living Peaceably One with Another" (1723)

Jonathan Edwards preached "Living Peaceably" at about age twenty in Bolton, a Connecticut River Valley farm village where he served as minister from fall 1723 to spring 1724. Bolton was not far from East Windsor, Edwards's birthplace and the town where his father, Timothy Edwards, was a prominent and influential minister. Timothy may in fact have engineered the Bolton appointment for his son.

The importance of Christian community was not a new subject for Edwards even this early in his career. He preached a similar message—the need for justice and beneficence, the importance of the common good, the virtue of unity—to his first congregation in lower Manhattan, following the completion of his undergraduate studies at Yale College. The Bolton sermon expanded on these themes. A community whose members help one another, tolerate those who disagree, and stand ready to forgive and love its adversaries will enjoy greater prosperity, more happiness, higher reputation, and the prospect of not only collective holiness but individual salvation. Living peaceably is God's will and Christ's way, and is therefore a Christian duty that extends to all of humanity, whatever their beliefs or however they look.

There are several rhetorical and argumentative devices in "Living Peaceably" that Edwards would use repeatedly: Christ as a model of behavior; rhapsodic descriptions of nature; humanity's biological unity and need for society; the listing of possible objections and Edwards's responses; an itemized guide to Christian behavior. Notable, too, is his reliance on the reason and experience of his parishioners, their "reasonableness," and the mandate of scripture.

Edwards left Bolton after a few months to become a tutor at Yale, where he could work toward a graduate degree (and possibly distance himself from the watchful eyes of his formidable father). But leaving Bolton did not mean jettisoning his ardor for Christian community, which would recur with great force throughout his life.

From *The Works of Jonathan Edwards*, vol. 14, *Sermons and Discourses, 1723–1729*, ed. Kenneth P. Minkema (New Haven: Yale University Press, 1997), 116–33.

If it be possible, as much as lieth in you, live peaceably with all men.
(Romans 12:18)

This chapter [Romans] is a sort of a summary of those virtues and graces, amiable actions and heavenly dispositions, which more especially adorn the Christian, and make 'em shine brighter than other men. If the rule of this chapter were but followed universally in the world, it would most surprisingly transform and alter it, and make it another in comparison, but little differing from Jerusalem. The chapter is well worth our most diligent and frequent reading, and that we should bind the words and rules thereof, that we should bind them upon our hearts . . . as by an excellent catalog of those duties and practices, which, if performed, will make us appear Christians indeed, and will mold our hearts and regulate our lives according to Jesus Christ and his image. . . .

Here are directions for behavior with relation unto men, which exceedingly tend to make mankind happy, and to make each particular person both excellent and blessed in human and Christian society, and every particular society to flourish. . . .

Here we are exhorted to distribute to the necessity of saints, and to be given to hospitality; to bless them by whom we are wronged and abused; to bless always and never to curse; to sympathize with others, either in their prosperity or adversity, from love to them; and to rejoice with those that do rejoice, and weep with those that weep, as if their prosperity were our own. This is not only our friends, but if we would be as Christians, we must rejoice at the happiness of those that persecute us, and weep and be grieved for their misfortunes. Here we are exhorted to unanimity, and to be of the same mind one towards another; not to mind high things, but to condescend [get on the same level] to men of low degree, those that are below ourselves, and not to be wise in our own conceit; to recompense [retaliate] to no man for evil, and to provide things honest in the sight of all. . . . If men did use themselves to be kind unto those that abused them, to bless those that persecuted them, and did not mind high things, but were humble and lowly, and would condescend one to another, and were not wise in their own conceits—that is, if they were not tenacious of their own opinions, as thinking themselves wiser than any other—if men were slower in resenting injuries, and would never recompense evil for evil, and would be fair and open and sincere in all their dealings, and honest in the sight of the world, there would need no more in order to obtaining peace with all men. . . .

We ought to endeavor to live peaceably with all men universally. None are to be excepted. The gospel spirit is a catholic spirit, a noble and unconfined benevolence, like unto that of our Creator, not confined to any particular part of mankind exclusive of others; but the Christian's good will is general to all the seed of Adam. 'Tis in this respect like the beams of the sun that enlightens the whole world and rejoices all sorts of creatures, shines indifferently on gardens and the wilderness, on fruitful fields and the barren mountains alike, on fragrant fruits and flowers and on the bramble; or rather like to God, who causes his sun to rise and his rain to descend on the good and the bad. . . .

We ought to follow peace with unjust and sinful men as well as with those who are to appearances true Christians and the fearers of God. This we are to do by all lawful means. Not that we are to countenance them in any wickedness; yea, we ought to manifest zeal for the glory of God and interest of religion, and the utmost abhorrence of wickedness in whomsoever it is found, and to discountenance [disavow] such persons as are notorious sinners, to withdraw from them and not to company with them. But yet there is no need of our causing contention and strife upon their account, if it be possible to avoid it. We need not be at peace with their practices, but we may be at peace with their persons. To make the wickedness of men the cause of contention and strife in us, is to make one sin the cause of another. . . .

Alas, if we should take the liberty upon every occasion to fight and quarrel and contend with men from this excuse, that they are wicked men, the world would be full of nothing but fighting and strife and the most woeful confusion; and Christianity, instead of being the gospel of peace, would be the greatest incendiary of strife; for if we are to fight with all but godly men, how few are there but that we should contend with them.

We ought to endeavor to live in peace with those who are of different opinions from us. 'Tis a most unreasonable thing to take the liberty of contending with men because they cannot see with our eyes. If this were granted, we should be at war with the greatest part of the world. 'Tis as unreasonable to strive with others because they can't be in everything of our minds, as to quarrel with another because he differs in the color of his hair or the features of his face. . . .

Yes, if another man differs from us in the substantials and fundamentals of religion, however erroneous he is and however pernicious his tenets, yet we ought, as much as in us lies, to endeavor to live peaceably with him. Our text seems to be put in such universals terms, with an eye to the heathen amongst whom the Christians in those times lived: they are required, if it be possible, to live peaceably with them. And certainly, if differences in opinion with respect to religion ought not to be the cause of our not living peaceably with men, much less ought differences of opinion in other matters, however positive and assured we may be in any matter, and others will not think as we do and are as positive in the contrary opinion. How foolish and childish is it to break peace upon this account. . . .

Some say they do love them that do them wrong and wish them no hurt, but wish them well, that are mistaken: they have no sincere and hearty love to them, but would feel really the better for their misfortunes, would smile to hear that they met with as bad injuries as they did to them; not only because they hoped it would enlighten their eyes to see their souls for their own good but would really be secretly glad because evil is befallen them. They know not their own hearts. We ought to have a love that is true, inward and sincere to our injurers, whether they injure us in our estates, or names, or bodies; whether they injure us by one vice or another, whether by covetousness and a craving after much of the world, or by their malice or backbiting. . . .

We ought to endeavor to live peaceably with all men to the utmost of our power. We must do as much as is possible this way and as much as in us lies. That is, if anything that we can do tends to the establishing of peace with any, we ought to do it. We ought to study how we may maintain peace. Peace is a thing so excellent and desirable, and tends so much to our own and to others' happiness, that we ought to pursue it on that account; and then it is a thing so necessary, that we ought to seek it as we would seek the welfare of mankind, the prosperity of our souls. We must be active for peace, peacemakers as well as not peace-breakers. . . .

Some may say, "Let them that I am contending with follow those rules of the Word of God concerning living peaceably with all men. They would be willing to follow the rules if the opposite party would, but they will be bound to no such rules, but will take liberty to contend with me; and why not I with them? I shall but do by them as they by me."

To this I answer, What unreasonable arguing is this: "Because another will not follow the rules of the gospel, therefore I need not; because others do not obey the express commands of God, therefore I need not"? Does God say, "Do this if other men do it," or does he say positively, "Do it," without a condition? Does God mean so love your enemies if they'll love you? This is a contradiction, for if they followed the gospel with respects to us, and love us, they would be no more enemies but friends; and what thanks if we love our friends? . . . Does the New Testament say, "Do by others as they do by you"? or don't it rather say, "Do by others as you would that they should do by you"? Christ speaks positively without a condition: "But I say unto you, love your enemies." . . .

Some say, "If I should be kind to those who wrong me, they would not thankfully receive it nor take notice of it."

Ans. Do you obey the commands of God for the thanks of men, or because they are the commands of God? Are we not commanded to be kind unto the unthankful (Luke 6:35)? Or suppose, instead of being thankful for our kindness, they abused it and were the more unworthy. Why, if we should continue kindness to them notwithstanding, we should do more than follow the example of our Father in heaven, for multitudes of men do abuse his kindness. . . .

If we should do what in us lies to live peaceably with all men, we must forgive one another. If anything is done wherein we think another to blame, we ought to forgive and bury it in oblivion, and not to suffer all love to be broken on the account and hatred to prevail, if something is done whereby we are wronged and injured; and not only to forgive upon their manifestation of repentance and upon their acknowledgment, but although they should continue obstinate, and should finally persist in what they had done, we ought so far to forgive, or nevertheless to retain a hearty good will and readiness to do any kindness from the heart, so as to be neighborly towards him and peaceable with him. . . .

If we would do what in us lies for to live peaceably with men, we must in some cases forego our own private interest, yea, our own right, or the sake of peace. 'Tis one sort of suffering for the sake of Christ, who is the prince of peace, to suffer for the sake of peace and quietness. . . .

First. Let it be considered that we are all reasonable creatures. How exceeding unpleasant and undesirable is contention amongst reasonable creatures. 'Tis the part of beasts, of wolves, tigers, dogs and the beasts of the forest to bite and devour one another. 'Tis exceeding hateful amongst creatures that have reason and understanding, and of such a noble make.

Second. We are all made of the same blood. We are all descendants of the same heavenly Father who has made us all, and all from the same earthly father and mother; so that we are all brethren, of whatever nation, religion or opinion. Acts 17:26, "And hath made of one blood all nations of men." And shall we, who are brethren, contend and fight one with another?

Third. We are made one for another. We are not made for ourselves alone; we are made to be useful to society. Neither can we possibly subsist without the help of our fellow men. God in the creation designed men for society, that we might help each other and love each other; and shall we, instead of that, tear one another or do what tends to make each other's lives uncomfortable?

Fourth. Peaceableness betokens a noble and a generous disposition of mind. 'Tis a sign of a little mind, of an inferior soul, to be upon every occasion picking a quarrel and flying out at everyone. But he that is of a noble disposition is not so lavish of his passion. He rather disdains to be moved to anger by unworthy men. He is of a generous disposition and freely condescends and yields to others, is not presumptuous and self-willed as those spoken of, II Peter 2:10. Peaceableness is the effect of considerateness and a capacious mind.

Fifth. Let it be considered how much it tends to make our lives happy, to live peaceably with all men. 'Tis the contrary that makes our lives in this world unpleasant. How happy are they who live in peace and unity: it makes all troubles seem the less, and makes the world easy to us. We cannot consult our own happiness more than by endeavoring to live peaceably with all men. All happiness consists in peace. There is no happiness of no kind but what is derived in peace, either peace with our fellow creatures or peace of conscience, peace in our own minds or peace with God. All happiness on earth and all happiness in heaven consists in peace, and all evil consists in contention, either contention with ourselves, fellow creatures, or God. Even bodily pain is the result of contention, even contention and struggle of nature with the painful sensation.

Therefore "peace" is put very often in Scripture for all manner of good. It was the usual salutation, "Peace be with you," thereby intending their desires of their good and happiness in general. . . .

Sixth. Consider how often and how positively 'tis commanded in those places of Scripture which have been already mentioned, and in many others it is vehemently urged and much insisted, and the neglect of it much blamed. If we pretend anything about the Word of God, let us consider what we find in it and practice. . . .

Seventh. Consider that this peaceable spirit is necessary in order to salvation. Those duties are not only convenient, as they are often thought. Those things are of greater importance than is often thought, not only virtues that belong to eminent saints but to every true Christian, and what 'tis impossible to obtain heaven without.

2

Miscellanies Notebook: "The Millennium" (1723, 1726)

In 1723, Edwards began a lifelong habit of recording his observations and thoughts in *Miscellanies* notebooks. These became a main repository for doctrinal and social analysis and speculation on, for example, the Trinity, conversion, secular and church government, other writers, nature, and passages of scripture. No book of the Bible intrigued him more than Revelation, with its predictions of an apocalypse, an end time that would bring not only Christ's Second Coming and a sorting of saved and damned at the Last Judgment, but also, in a long period prior to that Second Coming, a millennial (literally "thousand-year") era of holy Christian community.

Many Puritans of the seventeenth century, born of a violent, revolutionary tradition, were "premillennialists" who believed that the Second Coming would precede the millennium—that it almost *had* to precede it given the current state of human depravity. But a growing number of Puritans, from Thomas Brightman at the end of the sixteenth century to John Cotton in the seventeenth century, began to expect a period of progressively increasing blessings for the church and the gradual destruction of its enemies *before* the millennium and return of Christ. At the beginning of the eighteenth century, many commentators on the end times wrote that as the world neared its end, God's true church would prosper and God's enemies would be chastised. Then at some later point, the perfect millennial prosperity of the church would begin. Only after that would Christ physically return to earth. This view was "postmillennialism," for it held that Christ would return after the end of the millennium. Edwards and these other postmillennialists studied the book of Revelation to determine what the millennium would actually be like and, more importantly, what signs there might be that its preparatory blessings were on the horizon.

The two *Miscellanies* excerpts below show Edwards's thinking on this question while he was in his twenties, a stage of his life when, as we have seen in his "Living Peaceably" sermon, he was somewhat optimistic about spiritual and social progress. The path to the "happy" millennium clearly lay in everyone everywhere coming to adore the Creator and becoming a single body in Christ, a position that seems to anticipate a powerful evangelical (meaning, for Edwards, Reformed Protestant) expansion. Equally clearly, he connected the advent of

From *The Works of Jonathan Edwards*, vol. 13, The "Miscellanies," a–500, ed. Thomas A. Schafer (New Haven: Yale University Press, 1994), 212–13, 369.

millennial society with improved technology, advances in learning of all kinds, and greater material well-being. He seemed also to anticipate a substantial, even startling, amount of regional, racial, and cultural diversity, though this, too, had been implicit in "Living Peaceably" and other early sermons.

"Terra Australis Incognita" was the legendary term for a great unknown southern continent. "Wild Tartary" was a reference to northern and central Asia, known in the eighteenth century for the Mongol Empire. "Hottentots" was the word used at that time for people who lived in what is now Botswana and South Africa.

Entry 26. How happy will that state be, when neither divine nor human learning shall be confined and imprisoned within only two or three nations of Europe, but shall be suffused all over the world, and this lower world shall be all over covered with light, the various parts of it mutually enlightening each other; when the most barbarous nations shall become as bright and polite as England; when ignorant heathen lands shall be stocked with most profound divines and most learned philosophers; when we shall from time to time have the most excellent books and wonderful performances brought from one end of the earth and another to surprise us—sometimes new and wondrous discoveries from Terra Australis Incognita, admirable books of devotion, the most divine and angelic strains from among the Hottentots, and the press shall groan in wild Tartary—when we shall have the great advantage of the sentiments of men of the most distant nations, different circumstances, customs and tempers; [when] learning shall not be restrained [by] the particular humor of a nation or their singular ways of treating of things; when the distant extremes of the world shall shake hands together and all nations shall be acquainted, and they shall all join the forces of their minds in exploring the glories of the Creator, their hearts in loving and adoring him, their hands in serving him, and their voices in making the world to ring with his praise.

Entry 262. 'Tis probable that this world shall be more like heaven in the millennium in this respect, that contemplative and spiritual employments, and those things that more directly concern the mind and religion, will be more the saints' ordinary business than now. There will be so many contrivances and inventions to facilitate and expedite their necessary secular business that they shall have more time for more noble exercises, and that they will have better contrivances for assisting one another through the whole earth, by a more expedite and easy and safe communication between distant regions than now. The invention of the mariner's compass is one thing by God discovered to the world for that end; and how exceedingly has that one thing enlarged and facilitated communication! And who can tell but that God will yet make it more perfect; so that there need not be such a tedious voyage in order to hear from the other hemisphere, and so the countries about the poles need no longer to lie hid to us but the whole earth may be as one community, one body in Christ

3

Images of Divine Things (1738)

Edwards, like centuries of Christian thinkers before him, practiced "typology," a method of analysis that saw Old Testament figures or events as anticipating New Testament events, thereby showing God's overall purpose in constructing and guiding the world. Edwards, going much further, interpreted the configurations of the natural material world as "shadows" or "images" of the spiritual world of God, thus demonstrating God's purpose in the whole of creation as well as human history.

Edwards started a journal in 1728, shortly after arriving in Northampton, where he recorded his thoughts on such "images of things divine." Entry 8 gives his reasoning: God created and sustains the material universe on the basis of order, harmony, and beauty, and therefore, by analogy, the spiritual world as well. Entry 79 offers a dramatic example of this and, by extension, a striking potential social application. All bodies in the universe, according to Edwards, an avid early student of Isaac Newton, are held together by gravity, one part thus benefiting another, the whole showing order, beauty, and harmony—which is a type of love or charity.

In entry 99, written about 1738, Edwards used the origins, growth, and fruition of trees of different kinds, mostly drawn from scripture, as types (figures or events) of the church of God. Trees change with the season, sometimes thriving, sometimes dying—but then return to thriving again. And so the church from age to age will constantly, under the care of good husbandmen, expand its head and stock (Jesus) and scatter its seeds in a "beautiful" and "lively" profusion. The church, despite setbacks, will grow in harmony and loveliness. Nature, if only dimly, shows us this.

Entry 8. It is apparent and allowed that there is a great and remarkable analogy in God's works. There is a wonderful resemblance in the effects which God produces, and consentaneity [mutual agreement] in his manner of working in one thing and another throughout all nature. It is very observable in the visible world. Therefore 'tis allowed that God does purposely make and order one thing to be in an agreeableness and har-

From *The Works of Jonathan Edwards,* vol. 11, *Typological Writings,* ed. Wallace E. Anderson and Mason I. Lowance, Jr. (New Haven: Yale University Press, 1993), 53, 81, 89.

mony with another. And if so, why should not we suppose that he makes the inferior in imitation of the superior, the material of the spiritual, on purpose to have a resemblance and shadow of them? We see that ever in the material world God makes one part of it strangely to agree with another; and why is it not reasonable to suppose he makes the whole as a shadow of the spiritual world?

Entry 79. The whole material universe is preserved by gravity, or attraction, or the mutual tendency of all bodies to each other. One part of the universe is hereby made beneficial to another. The beauty, harmony and order, regular progress, life and motion, and in short, all the well-being of the whole frame, depends on it. This is a type of love or charity in the spiritual world.

Entry 99. A tree that has so many branches from one stock and root, that gradually increases more and more, becomes so great in so manifold branches, twigs, leaves, flowers, fruit, from so small a seed and a little twig, appearing so beautiful and flourishing under the light of the sun and influences of the rain, is a lively image of the church of God, which is often compared to it in the Scripture. It is represented by an olive tree, and vine, and a palm tree, and the bush on Mt. Sinai, trees of lignaloes [spicy wood], cedar tree, etc. The church in different ages is lively represented by the growth and progress of a tree; and the church in the same age, in Christ its head and stock, is like a tree.

The various changes of a tree in different seasons, and what comes to pass in its leaves, flowers and fruit in innumerable instances that might be mentioned, is a lively image of what is to be seen in the church. The ingrafting of a tree and the various things done about it by the husbandmen also represent what is to be seen in the church. There is a marvelous representation of the abundant profusion of God's goodness and lovely grace in what is to be seen in a tree, therein representing what is to be seen in the church. Some particular sorts of trees do more represent the church on some accounts, and others on others, as the vine, the olive, the palm, the apple tree, etc. A tree also is many ways a lively image of a particular Christian, with regard to the new [reborn, saved] man, and is so spoken of in Scripture.

4

Sermon: "Sin and Wickedness Bring Calamity and Misery" (1729)

In 1727, Edwards moved with Sarah, his new wife, to the Connecticut River town of Northampton, Massachusetts, to become assistant minister to his grandfather Solomon Stoddard, one of the best-known Congregational preachers in New England. When Stoddard died two years later, Edwards took over as fulltime minister. He remained there until the middle of the century.

"Sin and Wickedness" was a "fast day" sermon, designed to remind his audience, including judges and other officials of the local county court, that God's covenant with New England required proper behavior and leadership as well as staunch faith. The sermon warned against wickedness that would imperil not only individuals but communities and "our country," Great Britain. He took a swipe at heavy drinking and gross sensuality on the grounds that they were likely to weaken colonial defenses. He condemned ignorance as an impediment to a full understanding of Christian virtues and common moral law. But his most vigorous attacks were against worldliness, pride, and greed, which threatened to shatter trust and lead to corrupt, unjust government. The pride and covetousness of those in authority were especially dangerous since people naturally looked up to and emulated authority figures.

Here, too, Edwards itemized the points he wanted to make. This was a preaching technique that Puritan ministers like Edwards used to help parishioners remember the sermon. His language was unusually vivid—"wickedness," "corruption," "injustice," "barbarous," "inhuman," "stupidity"—which went somewhat against his insistence on civility, social harmony, and love. His main concern was with public well-being rather than individual souls. He believed, like many before him, that God deals both with individuals and with whole societies. The righteousness of an entire society would be rewarded by God, and its sins would be punished by God. Since ministers had responsibility not only for individual souls but also for the little societies of their towns and parishes, sometimes strong language was needed. This meant, in Edwards's view, that ministers needed to speak truth to both authority and the public, even if that meant criticizing, at least implicitly, persons of high standing who broke the covenant and moral law and betrayed the public interest.

From *The Works of Jonathan Edwards*, vol. 14, *Sermons and Discourses, 1723–1729*, ed. Kenneth P. Minkema (New Haven: Yale University Press, 1997), 484–505.

Righteousness exalteth a nation: but sin is a reproach to any people.
(Proverbs 14:34)

This verse, as most of the rest of these divine proverbs, consists of opposite predications [logical statements] on opposite qualities and persons. Here we may observe,

The two opposite qualities are righteousness and sin. The righteousness spoken of, being a public righteousness, may be extended so far as to take in all moral virtues and external religion, as well as sincere holiness; and sin is to be understood in a sense answerable for what is opposite to both. . . .

When a nation is greatly weakened and impoverished and brought into decaying, languishing, calamitous circumstances, they [members] become the object of reproach and contempt among their neighbors. Sin, as it brings 'em to this, is a reproach to any people. . . .

When such manners and ways of living as are inconsistent with external morality are common amongst a people, then wickedness may be said to prevail. . . . When vice overruns a land or town, and becomes a common thing; when the restraints of reputation and the conscience and the laws of men are commonly despised and broke over; when sensuality, profaneness and injustice prevail, then a people may be said to be a wicked people. . . .

When wickedness and immorality is countenanced or winked at by those whose business it is to suppress it, viz. by the rulers of a people, either civil or ecclesiastical: when civil rulers don't take due care to make good laws against immorality or don't take due care to execute the laws, don't show a zeal against iniquities, are no terrors to evildoers; when the reins of civil government are let loose, and wicked men can be open and barefaced with impunity; ministers don't bear a testimony; and when ecclesiastical discipline is not upheld, but scandalous persons are allowed to come to the Lord's table and to enjoy other privileges of visible Christians. . . .

When wickedness prevails amongst rulers, it argues a general corruption, because they follow example.

When public affairs are wickedly managed, when rulers ben't faithful to the glory and honor of God and the interest of the people that they are set to rule over.

When they seek their own private interest more than the interest of the public; when all their aim is to enrich and advance themselves; when they will make the public weal give place to their own private designs.

When they rule unjustly, oppressing the innocent or justifying the guilty.

When they are not impartial in judging, but are more influenced by favor or affection than the justice of the cause. . . .

Sin tends to the temporal ruin of particular persons, but much more inevitably to the ruin of a public society; not only as it directly hurts the particular members, but as it weakens and breaks the bonds of union instead of making a people subservient to one another's good, which is the end of society.

The temporal welfare of a people consists in these following things, viz. in their health and longevity, in their wealth, in their strength and ability to defend themselves, in their peace, in the prevalency of common justice, in public good order and government, in civility and decency. Each of which the prevailing of sin and wickedness amongst a people directly tends to destroy. . . .

Men's vices often prove very costly things to 'em. How much of the wealth and treasure of the world is expended in this corrupt age in nothing but that which is altogether needless and also very hurtful? How much is expended yearly in this land, for instance, to gratify a useless appetite after strong drink, that might be reserved to be expended much more to the profit of the owners and more for the good of the public?

Vice prevailing greatly weakens a people and makes them far less able to uphold and defend themselves. It weakens them as it enfeebles their bodies, and so renders them the more unfit for the fatigue and hardship and warlike achievements necessary for the defense of a nation. . . .

Thus sin is a reproach to any people, as they thereby lose their power and influence, and so lose their honor and expose themselves to the contempt and the insults of their neighbors; and often by this means are reduced from a prosperous and flourishing state, to become subjects and slaves to foreigners' honor. . . .

The more wickedness prevails, the less will those rules of the gospel about meekness, peaceableness, forgiving injuries, not suffering the sun to go down upon our wrath, loving our neighbors as ourselves, loving and blessing our enemies, bearing one another's burdens, looking every one not only at his own things, but every one also at the things of others. . . .

Men will look every one at his own separate interest, and that will be what will govern him. Whence will abundance of contention arise, it being only their own wealth and their own honor that they look at. They will be ready to envy their neighbors, and will be tempted to seek their own interest. . . .

The prevalency of wickedness tends to overthrow common justice between one man and another.

The welfare of a people depends very much upon this. If this ben't upheld, men can't subsist one by another. There is no living in society without the observation of common justice and honesty. The safety of men's lives and fortunes, reputations, all their outward possessions, depends upon it. If this were not observed, men would be each other's devourers; they would be like wolves one to another.

But so much the more as sin and wickedness prevails, so much the less will this be upheld, for men will have so much the less of the restraint of religion and conscience; and if men's consciences don't restrain them, there is nothing else will be sufficient to keep them from injuring and doing violence one to another. They will do their neighbors any injury whereby they can any way advantage or gratify themselves. Whenever there is the advantage of secrecy and hopes of not being discovered, men won't scruple to break promises or to take false oaths. Men would not be able to live quietly one by another, because they could put no trust in one another.

It tends to confound government and good order. Good rulers will not be likely to be found, nor a people be so likely to be unanimous in choosing those that would rule well, if they have to do in choosing of them.

Rulers would be likely to be unfaithful, to oppress those under their power and government, to seek only their own private interest at the expense of the public and not to be governed by principles of justice. So much the less will there be of distributive justice. Rulers will turn betrayers of the people's interests.

The subjects, or the ruled, will not pay that obedience and submission to authority, but will be rebellious and treacherous towards those that are set over them.

An oath, that is so necessary an instrument in government, would be the less regarded.

Ministers and people, and so the very end of people's being united in civil or ecclesiastical societies, will be overthrown, and what was intended for the good of mankind will turn to their hurt.

It tends to destroy humanity, civility and common decency. The temporal welfare of a people in great measure consists in these things. A people that are barbarous, inhuman and uncivilized, they are a miserable people. It is a misery for mankind to live together like beasts, with the like stupidity, ignorance and roughness as they; it is a calamity in mankind to be debased in their dispositions and manner below the dignity of the human nature.

But the prevalency of sin and wickedness amongst a people tends more and more to introduce this. Humanity, civility, common decency and religion are so near akin, that if one prevails, the other will prevail, and if the one languishes, the other will decay with it. Beastly lusts, when they get head, will make men of a beastly disposition and behavior all over, especially if they have not those restraints of shame and fear of human punishment, as those restraints are generally greatly weakened. As wickedness generally prevails, wickedness grows bold and barefaced.

The prevailing of wickedness tends to the declining of common civility, as it tends to ignorance. A brutish ignorance will prevail if vice prevails, for men will neglect to seek after knowledge, especially that that is divine or moral, which they find no way subserves to their lusts. Education will be neglected, and children will grow up like the brute creatures, without instruction, and will be answerably barbarous in their manners. . . .

'Tis God's manner to bring calamities and misery upon a people in judgment for the prevalency of {wickedness amongst them}.* 'Tis as God has threatened in his holy Word: God rewards a public righteousness with public rewards and punishes public iniquity with {public judgments}, which can be done only in this world. In another world, mankind will be rewarded and punished only as particular persons, for

---

*Braces are used, as in the Yale edition of *The Works of Jonathan Edwards,* to fill in repeated phrases that Edwards represented with a long dash.

the bonds by which they are united in societies will then be dissolved. Though the guilt of all the sin that is in a nation lies upon particular persons, so that it will all be punished in another world, yet a people are punished as a people only in this world, though it may be with spiritual judgments. The prosperity or adversity of a people in this world is much more universally according to the prevalence {of wickedness amongst them} than {the wickedness} of a particular person.

We hence learn what cause we have to lament the prevalency of sin and wickedness in our nation. As we are a part of the nation, or of the same body politic, we ought to look upon ourselves as concerned in their guilt and in their calamity. If the nation is subject to calamities and is brought low, our interest is so much embarked with theirs, that we shall feel it as a member feels the disease of the head. We ought therefore greatly to lament the wickedness of the nation. . . .

Religion is less and less our business and concern; the world engrosses the thought and concern and talk of the land, and profaneness and pride and sensuality lift up their head, are very common and appear more and more openly and barefaced.

1. Profaneness. Profaneness consists in a behavior that shows a contempt of holy things, and is particularly opposite to that part of our duty that immediately relates to the worship and service of God. "Profane" signifies "common," being that whereby men treat sacred things as though they were common things and deserved no special regard. . . .

2. Pride and vanity. How excessively do many affect to make a flaunting appearance in their buildings and apparel and way of living, many going far beyond their condition or what would be suitable for them? They exercise their care about outward ornaments, which ought to be employed about the ornaments of the mind. . . .

3. Covetousness. How exceedingly does this prevail; how indefatigable are men in endeavoring to increase their estates, to grow rich and great; how busily are they employed? What a stir do they make about it, while they neglect their own souls and the souls of their children! How evident is it by but a little acquaintance and a slight view of the land, to see that the world is what men make their great concern?

If men live wicked lives, the guilt of prevailing iniquity amongst the people among whom they dwell is in proportion to their influence, whether it comes by their being in offices civil or ecclesiastical, or whether it be by their riches, or their reputations for learning or wisdom, or their being of an extensive relation or acquaintance. . . .

God is able to save us from this great calamity. If we can do nothing else towards a reformation, we can cry to God. Let us do it not only on fast days, but let it be the continual prayer of all who mourn for the transgressions of the land, and that have the interest of religion, the glory of God, and the public prosperity at heart.

5

Sermon: "Envious Men" (1730)

Edwards preached "Envious Men" on a sacrament day to celebrate the Lord's Supper, a significant event for New England Congregationalists since communion was only celebrated a few times a year. Edwards had said earlier in "Sin and Wickedness" that the sacrament table should be an occasion for Christian unity and cohesion, and that probably not everyone belonged there. He argued here that envy, one of the "deadly" sins of church tradition, especially has no place because envy is a kind of status-seeking, a "lust" for wealth or reputation and a resentment of those who have or might acquire it—a worldly obsession that is contrary to the life of the mind and spirit.

Also, said Edwards, envy rends the fabric of the community. Envy stems at times from the pettiest of personal behavior—backbiting, lying, fraud, false witness, unfair gossip, sheer spite—which spills over into public affairs, business dealings, or church activities. Envy drives people apart, creates dissension, causes mistrust, weakens communal bonds, frays the ties of neighborliness, and besmirches a community's reputation and collective identity. Envy is, therefore, a social as well as a personal sin, and all the more reprehensible because of that.

Edwards, here as always an acute reader of the human condition, cautioned that envy is an individual psychological disorder. The envious are continually anxious lest their neighbor either have too much of some desirable thing—wealth, raiment, reputation, education, even spirituality or happiness—or else acquire it too quickly and easily. The envious fret and worry, cannot rest, and thus experience psychic as well as spiritual pain. They know neither peace nor joy nor comfort.

In the public arena, Edwards implied, criticism may be valid, even necessary. But people should search their hearts to make sure their criticism is just and honest and in the public interest, not a mere platform for personal revenge, jealousy, or ambition. It is a fine line that, as always with Edwards, needs faith and spiritual guidance to follow.

From *The Works of Jonathan Edwards*, vol. 17, *Sermons and Discourses, 1730–1733*, ed. Mark Valeri (New Haven: Yale University Press, 1999), 101–20.

TEXT. *For where envying and strife is, there is confusion and every evil work.* (James 3:16)

Envy is a being grieved or uneasy of another's prosperity, as if the prosperity of another be the thing that hurts a man and makes him feel uneasy or unpleasantly. That is envy, of whatever kind that prosperity is, whether it be spiritual or temporal prosperity. . . .

Envy evermore arises from self-love and a want of loving our neighbor as ourselves. Some envy others because their prosperity is greater than theirs; they can't bear to see others above 'em. And a man may envy another whose prosperity is not so great as his own. It may come too near an equality with it for him to be easy with it; though he is something above his neighbor, yet he loves to be more above him than he is. Thus the elder brother [in the parable of the prodigal son] envied the younger because his father killed the fatted calf for him, though, as his father told him, he was always with him and all that he had was his (Luke 15:31).

This envy is a thing of a very pernicious tendency, when it only lurks in a man's heart and puts forth itself in inward exercises, if it don't break out into outward actions. All men have this principle of corruption in them, but some are much more in the exercise of it than others. Where there is much of the workings of an envious spirit in man's heart, it is like poison to him. The prevalency of such lusts is like a viper at the heart of religion. Religion never will, never can, flourish in a heart where envy is indulged; it is exceeding contrary to Christianity.

And then it is an uncomfortable sort of passion. What we have said of the nature of it evidences this; the nature of it consists in grief and uneasiness. It destroys a man's comfort to be of an envious disposition. He goes about fretting himself and having pain and uneasiness at those things that he has no sort of occasion to be uneasy of. He can't enjoy himself because his neighbor prospers. If he would be easy and quiet about the condition of other men, he would be in far better condition himself; he would enjoy himself a great deal better.

And if he restrains himself and his envy don't break out into open contention, yet if there be a great deal of the exercises of it in a man's breast, it will show itself in some way or other: He won't perform those duties towards his neighbor that he should do, and he will not be forward to promote his good. He will inwardly rejoice at his misfortunes.

It will be agreeable to him to hear him talked against; he'll hear it with pleasure. . . .

It is of very pernicious consequence to the persons contending: it is especially pernicious unto them. The man that from envy contends with his neighbor and shows his ill will to him, and spite against him, he don't hurt his neighbor one-tenth part so much as himself. He foolishly bites himself out of envy and spite to another. He endeavors to send his darts against his neighbor; when indeed he stabs them into himself. He gives himself abundantly the worst wounds.

1. He destroys his own peace and comfort. He disturbs the calm and repose of his own mind; by the heats of his spirit he is put into a tumult. There is as much difference between him whose spirit is disturbed by envy and malice and contention, and a man that is of a meek and quiet spirit, as there is at sea when it is calm, and the surface of the water is smooth, and the sky clear and the heavens serene, and when there is a storm, and the water and the winds are all in a rage, and the heavens covered with black clouds. The envious, contentious man's mind can't rest. . . .

2. Envious contention contracts abundance of guilt; God exceedingly hates such things. 'Tis very contrary to the nature of true holiness and the nature of God; God is a God of love and of peace. And how much has he insisted upon the duties of love in his holy Word! 'Tis exceeding contrary to the nature of Christ, the Lamb of God. Men are not sensible how guilty they are before God by their strife and envy. . . .

When such a spirit prevails, many lusts are in exercise. When a man's spirit is heated with envy and a spirit against others, all the whole gang of lusts, they rise. There is pride; men never show their pride so much as in contention. There is intemperate wrath. There is revenge. There is covetousness, for when they contend it is about the world generally, and raises and puts into exercise a covetous spirit. And there is injustice. So, when men's spirits are heated in contention, they han't regard to justice; they ben't wont to tie up themselves to rules. They han't coolness of spirit enough to consider [whether] what they do is just or unjust.

Contention puts the soul into an exceeding ill frame. . . .

Envy and strife are of exceeding pernicious consequences in any society. When any society are got into a contention, and there are envyings, emulations, wrath, strife in the society, or when there is such a spirit shown publicly and in the management of public business, 'tis of very pernicious consequences.

1. It destroys the comfort of society. God has made man with such a nature that he is fitted and inclined to live in society, and he is of such a nature and circumstances that we are necessitated to dwell in society. And society, if well improved, tends much to the happiness of mankind. But the comfort of society very much consists in love and peace; Psalms 133:1, "Behold, how good and how pleasant it is for brethren to dwell together in unity!" Especially it should be accounted so amongst a Christian people.

2. It makes confusion in a society. As it is said in our text, "Where there is envy and strife, there is confusion." Contention puts things in an uproar; it confounds that good order which is the beauty of society. It frequently occasions many indecencies. Men in the heat of their passion don't keep themselves within the bounds of decency and good order; they'll vent their spirit and don't regard what becomes of decency. . . .

3. 'Tis to a people's dishonor. Such things are soon famed [talked about] abroad.

4. The prevailing of envy and contention exceedingly hinders the success of ordinance and the flourishing of religion amongst a people. When a people are contending, religion evermore runs very low. . . .

5. In a society where there is contention, there is every evil work; that is, it has a tendency to promote every ill thing. There will be evil speaking, backbiting; men will get together and spend away their evenings in talking against their neighbor, setting forth his ill qualities and telling of the ill things he has done. They feed one another with such talk. . . .

Where there is envying and contention, ten to one but there will be misrepresentations of things and lying, carried on without end by one or other. There will be slandering; there will be abundance of false reports spread about that have been raised by one busybody or other.

Sometimes envy and contention is the occasion of abominable cheating. Men will take fraudulent, knavish, vile methods to accomplish their designs, and to get their wills, and to carry their purposes against those that they envy. . . .

Examine your own heart. Is it out of pure love to your country and tender concern for its welfare that you are concerned that such persons are in such and such honorable or profitable posts? Is that indeed the very thing; is it only that, or is it that chiefly? Or is not this the truth of the case: that 'tis the person's honor or prosperity that is the very spring; of your concern and uneasiness? Would it not be agreeable to you, and what you would in your heart be glad of, if he should be deprived of it, though it should not be at all more for the interests and welfare of the country? Be plain and ingenuous in confessing the matter as it really is to your own conscience.

Do you verily think that your uneasiness at such and such man's advancement and profit, and others that are of the same spirit with you is only or chiefly out of a public spirit and a peculiar love to your country and concern for its welfare that you are of more than other men? Would you not be glad, though your country suffered as much another way? Or is it not envy; is not the prosperity of their persons the main thing with you? If you are a good man, you'll bear to be searched.

Again, it may be you'll say it is from love to justice. There are other men that deserve such posts it is but fitting they should have. And so you pretend that your uneasiness is only because you are concerned that other men may have their rights. Here again I desire you, see that you don't deceive yourself. . . .

It may be you'll say that their honor and prosperity hurts them. It makes 'em proud; they have too much sail; they are like to be overset with it. They advanced too high; they can't bear it; they grow so proud and assuming that there is no doing with them. And so you pretend that is it out of concern for them, for their good, that you are uneasy of their advancement. But is it so indeed? Is it really out of hearty and sincere love to 'em that you are concerned at their prosperity? Is not this a mere sham? Is it not the right reverse of love?

When will you ever find a man that envies another, but that he will have some such excuses and pleas for it? He'll say he is not fit, and he is proud, and it does him a great deal of hurt, and many things they'll say against those that they envy, as if they were worthy to be hated by everyone.

Examine yourself, whether or no you don't suffer your envy to break out in your talk and behavior: Is it not the occasion of a great deal of evil speaking? Is it not a thing that you allow yourself, to vent your envy in reproaching and reviling the men you envy? Don't you love to go and sit and talk with some others of the same party and the same spirit with yours, and spend your time in judging and declaiming against your neighbor?

Is not this the root and spring of heats of spirit, and anger, and contention in you? Has not this been the occasion of contentious talk?

Is not this the occasion of your opposing your neighbor? Oftentimes, men that envy another and have a spirit against him will oppose another in anything that he endeavors to promote for no other cause but only that he loves to vent his spite. He'll endeavor to hinder and clog him in any of his designs and undertakings, for no other reason. . . .

Sometimes there is so much of this spirit between parties in a place that there are many that regard the carrying on the particular designs of their party more than the greatest public good; it is very sorrowful when it is so.

Envy between parties is a passion that generally is not alone; there are others as bad as that, or at least much akin to it for badness, along with it. There is generally a spirit of revenge. There are old grudges. Men remember some old things that have passed long ago, some old affront they can't forget, and never will leave trying to come up with 'em for it. . . .

Consider how exceeding contrary such a spirit and practice is to the spirit of Christianity. The spirit of Christianity is a spirit of love and peace; Christ is the Prince of Peace. He abundantly insisted upon it, that his disciples should love one another. That was his commandment; hereby, he told 'em, all men should know his disciples from others, that they loved one another (John 13:34–35). This is the royal law, that we should love one another.

Christ himself, whose professed disciples we are, was meek and lowly, exceeding far from an envious and contentious spirit. He did not vex himself about this and that man's being promoted. . . .

Generally, those that are of an envious spirit and practice towards their neighbor are guilty of the very same things that they find fault with them for. Envious persons generally find fault with them they envy for their pride. They make that an excuse for their envy, that he is a proud man, and 'tis not fit that such a person should be advanced; it makes 'em still more proud and they want to be humbled, whereas they are guilty of the very same thing: they are proud, and thence comes their envy. They would not concern themselves who is advanced and who has honor, were it not for their pride; but their proud hearts can't bear to see their neighbor above them or it may be, not equal with them. They think their neighbor is proud, and intends to grow great, and to get above them, and they can't bear it; 'tis because of their pride. Otherwise, it would not hurt 'em at all. They would let him alone who would get honor; they would not concern themselves about it. . . .

Consider how much it destroys your own comfort here in this world. Which do you think is the happiest man? He that minds his own concerns, seeking his own salvation and eternal happiness, and is not uneasy at others' prosperity, has not his own calm at all disturbed, let who will be advanced; he that is willing to leave it with providence to promote whom God will to earthly honor and wealth? Or he that frets himself about such a man's getting money easily, and about his growing great, and for fear he will think himself bigger than he; he frets himself, it may be, about the honor that is put upon him, his being advanced to some post, or having a higher seat in the meeting house, or some such thing? "A sound heart is life of the flesh; but envy rottenness to the bones" (Proverbs 14:30).

6

Sermon: "The State of Public Affairs" (1731–32)

Edwards often preached social or political sermons on special occasions such as fast or communion days when he expected attendance to be higher than usual and might include magistrates or other visiting dignitaries. He delivered this sermon on a fast day that coincided with intense debates among Massachusetts Bay's leaders over policies—how to maintain the royal governor, deal with currency problems, and pay for a militia for a war with Spain—and also over broader constitutional issues such as the power of the colonial assembly, the right of colonial self-determination, and the sanctity of the colony's royal charter, which included provisions for religious freedom that mattered hugely to Congregational ministers.

Edwards used this occasion to offer parishioners an example of a wise statesman, King Solomon. Solomon loved God, according to Edwards, knew a lot about nature and men and manners, was skillful in politics and the art of government, and was devoted to the protection and well-being of his people. Edwards always celebrated learning, whether spiritual or secular, and praised it in Solomon. But Edwards also celebrated political skill and, by implication, politics itself. A people, he pointed out, must defend their rights and privileges from foreign conquest (by Spain or France), "powerful foes" from abroad (British authorities), and enemies "within" (colonial factions).

But dangers lurk, warned Edwards. Governments or rulers may change too frequently, which makes policy uncertain. There might be confusion about constitutional authority, which hinders decision-making. Secretiveness among rulers (by which he meant local or, here, provincial authorities) can cover up corruption and betrayal. Political conflict might stem from spite, jealousy, or ambition. This could lead to party tumult, which Edwards dreaded as much as James Madison or John Adams later would; to self-serving, avaricious rulers; and to the weakness and ruin of "the land" and "the people."

Edwards left room, somewhat surprisingly, for popular revolt against tyranny. He thought public opinion and "choosing" rulers were important, views that anticipated the republican thinking of the coming generation. He also called, as he often did, for greater piety, essential in his mind to keeping New England's covenant with God and thereby securing God's blessing. This idea of a "national

From *The Works of Jonathan Edwards*, vol. 17, *Sermons and Discourses, 1730–1733*, ed. Mark Valeri (New Haven: Yale University Press, 1999), 349–68.

covenant" reflects what we saw in an earlier selection (no. 4, "Sin and Wickedness Bring Calamity and Misery")—the notion that God deals with a whole society and not just individuals.

TEXT. *For the transgression of a land many are the princes thereof: but by a man of understanding and knowledge shall the state thereof be prolonged.* (Proverbs 28:2)

Ordinarily, great men are men of great understanding. Their greatness lies chiefly in eminency in some particular kind of knowledge. Some great men are great philosophers, others are great divines, others great statesmen. Solomon, of whom it is said that God gave him "wisdom and understanding exceeding much, and largeness of heart, even as the sand that is on the sea shore" (1 Kings 4:29), excelled in all kinds of knowledge. He was eminent for his knowledge in divinity, as is evident by the improvement which the Holy Ghost made of his wisdom in those divine writings of his that we have in our hands. . . .

He excelled greatly in philosophy as knowledge of nature. . . . He greatly excelled in his knowledge of the nature of the human soul. He excelled in his prudential knowledge of men and manners, as appears by his books of Proverbs and Ecclesiastes. He excelled in a practical genius . . .

But yet if there was any one part of wisdom wherein we can say he chiefly excelled, it must be politics, or his skill in the art of government. For this was especially that wisdom which Solomon asked of God. . . . He excelled in knowledge of things wherein the welfare of a community consisted, and in a discerning of the means for obtaining it. He knew what tended to the mischief and misery of a people, and what to their prosperity. . . .

One part of this verse [from Proverbs] explains the other. . . . A public calamity here mentioned in the former part, and the public blessing opposite thereto in the latter part. . . .

When the circumstances of a people are such that the continuance of a present establishment and of the rights and privileges which they thereby enjoy is doubtful, whether a people are threatened with this by the invasion of a foreign enemy, or are threatened with it by the supreme authority which they are under, or prove their own enemies and their privileges are in danger of being lost through their own imprudence and mismanagement.

This is the calamity that is directly spoken of in the text: the state of public affairs of a land being in a changeable posture, whereby a people are exposed to lose those rights, privileges, and public blessings which they enjoy by virtue of the present establishment; when a people are threatened with being deprived of their ancient privileges either in whole or in part and put under a new form of government; when the case is such that it is doubtful what of their civil enjoyments shall be continued to them, whether they ben't about to lose all their privileges or, if not what they shall not lose; when there are powerful enemies abroad that seek the eversion [turning inside out] of the state or enemies in a people's own bowels that are carrying on plots and designs against the present establishment, that they may have the better opportunity to advance their private interest or the interest of a party that they are attached to, or do it out of spite to any person or parties that they are enemies to.

When the persons in whose hands the government is often changed, this often arises from the unsettled state of public affairs; and if it don't arise from it, it has a tendency to it. . . .

When it is a matter undetermined and unsettled where the power of administration lies, then are the public affairs of a land in an unsettled state. When there are debates long maintained about privilege and prerogative, and matters of great importance to the government are long held in suspense because it is not determined who has powers of administration: in such a case the public affairs of a country are not settled on any foundation, because it is a thing as yet remains in suspense, on what foundation they ought to be settled upon.

When there is strife between different persons and parties for the power of government.

When there are many that would be princes and are contending together for the power; when the principal men of a country are designing men, are carrying designs one against another, each one to advance himself and to depress others; when the main struggle amongst the great men is who shall be uppermost and keep down the rest; when there is a spirit of jealousy amongst rulers one of another, and each one is suspicious of another lest he should have the most honor and influence in the government and accordingly are plotting to prevent him and to advance themselves; when the principal men don't make the public good but their own advancement their principal aim, and each one is striving to bring others into a dependence on him, and are for that end industriously insinuating themselves into the favor of the supreme power or striving for the favor and esteem of the people; when there are opposite parties among rulers each laboring to weaken the other and, as much as may be, to engross the power themselves; when the different orders of those who have the management of public business are not cemented, but one are jealous of another, and the lower orders are jealous lest the superior should take too much upon them and so should strive to keep them down, to get the power more into their hands; and the superiors, on the other hand, are jealous of the inferiors encroaching upon them and so are striving to get from them their privilege; when the people are striving with rulers, and rulers with people, and power become a bone of contention among them: then are the public affairs of a land in an unsettled state. . . .

The very excellency of a public state is its stability. The very end of men's uniting in a community is strength and firmness. This is the foundation on which we stand and on which our particular rights and privileges are built. And if this foundation be loose and unsettled, how miserable are we.

The unsettled state of public affairs commonly greatly interrupts the proceedings of public business. Things that need to be done are neglected, and the public in the meantime greatly suffers. The minds of those who have the care of public business are diverted by the changes, overturnings, and tumults there in public affairs. Rulers' minds are very much taken off from public business, and their time spent in those disputes and debates that arise.

Rulers are not so deeply engaged seeking the public good. They don't act with that strength and resolution, their own circumstances being unsettled and uncertain. And rulers, not being united among themselves, don't assist and strengthen one another, but rather weaken one another's hands.

Such an unsettled state is commonly attended with abundance of strife and contention, with jealousies and envyings. Rulers are divided into parties, and so the whole land with them. . . .

And such an unsettled state, if continued, tends to a people's ruin. It tends to its ruin from within and from without. The commonwealth is exposed, to become a prey to the ambition and avarice of men in its own bowels, of those that should be its fathers. The enemies of people that desire its overthrow have a great advantage given 'em hereby. It stirs up the public enemies; it awakens them to seek for an opportunity to make a prey of the country. They wish for its fall, and when they see it tottering they will be sure to put their shoulders to throw it down. . . .

Hence we may learn how much a people may wrong their posterity by their wickedness. The transgression of a people unsettles the state of a land and often puts an end to it, overthrows the privileges and rights which they enjoyed by virtue of a former establishment, which when lost are not easily recovered; so that not only the present, but future generations reap the bitter fruits of it. Their children and children's children may have cause to rue the transgressions of their fathers, whereby they are deprived of precious privileges which the land formerly enjoyed and which, had it not been for their forefathers' provocations, might have been handed down to them. . . .

But how little is there of self-reflection! How little is it considered that the unsettled and calamitous circumstances of the land is the judgment of God upon it for general corruption and the abounding wickedness of it. When we get into this humor of finding fault, 'tis fit that we should begin with ourselves, for here is the beginning of our calamities. What instruments soever are made use of, we should strike at the root. . . .

The state of the land that the wise man speaks of must be understood as containing some privilege. The case may be so, that it may be a blessing to have an end put to the state of a land; it may be so miserable that it may be a calamity to have it continued, as if a land is conquered by a foreign enemy and is in bondage under a cruel tyrant. . . . Now the continuance of such a state as this was not what the wise man meant by the state of a land's being prolonged, for such a state as this contains nothing of privilege in it. But by "the state of a land," 'tis evident the wise man intends a constitution whereby it has its power of government that it has within itself, and management of its own public affairs in a freedom from those whose interest is not united with theirs. . . .

We may observe how [God's] blessing is obtained: by a man of understanding and knowledge. By which the wise man don't mean only a subtile, cunning man; by understanding and knowledge is not meant merely state policy, for it is designing, crafty, political men that ordinarily are the instruments of overthrowing the state of a land, and their cunning will either tend to the prolonging of it or the overthrow of it according as they are well or ill inclined. But by a man of understanding and knowledge seems to be intended a man of righteousness or piety, though not exclusive of natural and moral wisdom and prudence, for these terms, wisdom or understanding, are generally so to be understood in this book for righteousness or piety. . . .

The righteous prolong the privileges of a land by their prayers. Their prayers are not only for themselves; they won't forget the people and land to which they belong when they make their addresses to God. They will deprecate the public calamities. . . .

When piety prevails among a people, it prevents the prevailing of ambition, and avarice, and self-seeking, and treachery among rulers that is very commonly the means by which the state of a land is unsettled and destroyed. When men have the fear of God before their eyes, they won't be governed by an aim to advance or enrich themselves more than the public good. They won't betray the public weal for private ends; they'll sincerely and conscientiously seek every one the good of the public. Their country may depend upon them. If they are wise and seeing and politic men, they will improve their policy to establish and advance the good of the land, and not to advance themselves and supplant others. The securing of the public peace will be their first care. . . .

'Tis a blessing that we should seek above all other public blessings that [God] would pour out his Spirit upon us. For 'tis by this that God gives a people knowledge and understanding; 'tis by this that God gives that blessing which lays a foundation for all other blessings. By this means we shall be reformed and religion and righteousness will be promoted amongst us. And this will procure for us, and secure to us, all manner of prosperity.

7

Sermon: "The Duty of Charity to the Poor" (1733)

"The Duty of Charity," preached in four parts in January 1733, was the longest sermon Edwards had yet delivered. The sermon articulated Edwards's communitarian values and sense of compassion, but did so in ways that, to some readers centuries later, appear to be harsh. Perhaps some of those in the pews on those icy winter days drew a similar conclusion. The sermon's length added weight to its message.

Edwards sometimes meant by "charity" an attitude of welcoming, acceptance, and affection. Here he meant something he thought was harder: giving money or goods to the needy. This is a Christian duty, he argued, as important as attending service or praying or reading the Bible. Such acts are powerful evidence, in fact the best public evidence, of sainthood. Greed and lack of compassion, by contrast, may reveal and "curse" you.

Wealth, Edwards reminded the congregation, belongs to God, the creator of all things, and since the poor, as the gospel tells us, are Christ's representatives, providing charity to the poor is simply returning wealth to its true owner. Jesus, who was himself poor, was a model of charity who gave his all in the end. Edwards insisted, as he had in earlier sermons, that human beings are of "one blood," made in God's image, in essence the same, and thus survive only through "society and union." And as society is essential to survival, charity is essential to society. Those looking out for themselves alone—later generations would use the term "individualists" or "libertarians"—deserve to be cast out.

Edwards anticipated many objections—eleven by one count—to this demanding argument and tried, sometimes at length, to respond to them. How do we know, for example, which poor people are truly needy? Find out if you can, but help too many rather than leave anyone in need. But what if we don't have enough for ourselves? Give anyway, unless you are genuinely poor, in which case giving will smack of pride. You probably only think you don't have enough, and if you don't, then God will provide. But shouldn't the poor ask directly for help? No, that would force them to become beggars and destroy their dignity. Well, doesn't the government help the poor? Yes, because in a fallen world, private charity is unreliable. But it helps, it shows grace and public purpose, and since God commands it, no one wanting to enter heaven is exempt.

From *The Works of Jonathan Edwards*, vol. 17, *Sermons and Discourses, 1730–1733*, ed. Mark Valeri (New Haven: Yale University Press, 1999), 369–404.

DOCTRINE: *'Tis the most absolute and indispensable duty of a people of God to give bountifully and willingly for the supply of the wants of the needy.*

'Tis the duty of a people of God to give bountifully. 'Tis commanded once and again in the text, "Thou shalt open thine hand wide unto him" (Deuteronomy 15:7–11). A merely giving something is not sufficient; it don't answer the rule or come up to God's holy command. But we must open our hand wide. . . .

'Tis the duty of a visible people of God to give for the supply of the needy freely, and without grudging. It don't at all answer the rule before God if it be done with an inward grudging; if the heart is grieved, and inwardly it hurts a man to give what he gives. . . .

This is a duty that a people of God are under very strict and indispensable obligations to. 'Tis not merely a commendable thing for a man to be kind and bountiful to the poor, but our bounden duty, as much a duty as 'tis to pray or go to meeting, or anything else whatsoever; and the neglect of it brings great guilt upon any person. . . .

And I know of scarce any particular duty that is so much insisted upon, so pressed and urged upon us, both in the Old Testament and New, as this duty of charity to the poor. . . .

For men are made in the image of God, and are worthy of our love upon this account. And then, we are all nearly allied to one another by nature: we have all the same nature, like faculties, like dispositions, like desires of good, like needs, like aversion to misery, and are made of one blood. And we are made to subsist by society and union, one with another, and God has made us with such a nature that we can't subsist without the help one of another.

Mankind in this respect are as the members of the natural body, are one, can't subsist alone without an union with and the help of the rest. Now, this state of mankind shows how reasonable and suitable it is that men should love their neighbors, and that we should not look every one at his own things, but "every man also on the things of others" (Philippians 2:4).

A selfish spirit is very unsuitable to the nature and state of mankind. He that is all for himself and none for his neighbors deserves to be cut off from the benefit of human society, and to be turned out among wild beasts, to subsist as well as he can. A private, niggardly spirit is more suitable for wolves and beasts of prey than for human beings.

Loving our neighbors as ourselves is the sum of the moral law respecting our fellow creatures, and helping of them and contributing to their relief is the most natural expression of this love. It is vain to pretend to a spirit of love to our neighbor when it grieves us to part with anything for their help when under calamity. They that love only in word and in tongue, and not in deeds, have no love in truth; any profession without it is a vain pretense. . . .

And then, Christ by his redemption has brought us into a more near relation one to another, hath made us children of God, children in the same family. We are all brethren, having God for our common Father, which is much more than to be brethren in any other family. He has made us all one body; therefore, we ought to be united, and subserve to one another's good, and bear one another's burdens, as members of the same body in the natural body. If one of the members suffers, all the other members bear the burden with it. . . .

Consider that what you have is not your own, i.e. you have no absolute right to it, have only a subordinate right. Your goods are only lent to you of God to be improved by you in such ways as God directs you. You yourselves are not your own. . . . And if you yourself are not your own, so then neither are your possessions your own. You have by covenant given up yourself and all you have to God; you have disclaimed and renounced any right in yourself, as in anything that you have, and given God all the absolute right. And if you are a true Christian, you have done it from your heart. . . .

So Christ teaches that we are to look upon our fellow Christians in this case as himself, and that our giving to or withholding from them shall be so taken as if we so behaved ourselves towards him. In Matthew 25:40, there Christ says to the righteous on his right hand who had supplied the wants of the needy, "In that ye have done it to one of the least of these my brethren, ye have done it unto me."

Now what stronger enforcement of this duty can be conceived, or is possible, than this, that Jesus Christ looks upon our kind and bountiful, or unkind and uncharitable, treatment of our needy neighbors as such as treatment of himself. If Christ himself was here upon earth and dwelt amongst us in a frail body, as he once did, and was in calamitous and needy circumstances, should not we be willing to supply him? Should we be apt to excuse ourselves from helping him? Should we not be willing to supply him, so that he might live free of distressing poverty? And if we did supply him, so that he might live free of distressing poverty? And if we did otherwise, should we not bring great guilt upon ourselves; might it not justly be very highly resented by God? Christ once was here in a frail body and stood in need of peoples' charity, and was maintained by it. . . .

Man is naturally governed only by a principle of self-love, and 'tis a difficult thing, to corrupt nature, for us men, to deny themselves of their present interest, trusting in God to make it up to them.

But how often has Christ told us the necessity of our doing difficult duties of religion: if we will be his disciples, then we must sell all, and take up our cross daily, to deny ourselves, to deny our own worldly profit and interest. . . .

It is a remarkable evidence how little many men realize the things of religion, whatever they pretend: either how little they realize that the Scripture is the Word of God, or, if it be, that he speaks true, that notwithstanding all the promises made to bounty to the poor in his Word, yet men are so backward to such duties, and are so afraid to trust God with a little of their estates. But observation may confirm the same thing that the Word of God teaches in this. It may be that God in his providence generally smiles upon and prospers those men that are of a liberal, charitable, bountiful spirit. . . .

Whether the time will ever come or not that we or our children shall be in pinching and distressing want of bread, yet, doubtless, evil will be on the earth. We shall have our times of calamity, wherein we shall stand in great need of God's pity and help, if not that of our fellow creatures. And God has promised that at such a time, he that has been of a charitable spirit and practice shall find help. . . .

We find many commands in Scripture to be charitable to the poor; the Bible is full of 'em; and you ben't excepted from those commands. God don't make any exception of any particular kinds of persons that are especially in danger of making a righteousness of what they do; and God often counsels and directs persons to this duty. Now, will you presume to say that God has not directed you to the best way? He has advised you to do thus, but you don't think it is best for you but would do you more hurt than good if you should do it. You think there is other counsel better than God's, and that 'tis the best way for you to go contrary to God's command. . . .

Again, some may object against charity to such or such particular persons, so that they are not obliged to give 'em charity, for though they are in need yet they ben't in extremity. 'Tis true, they meet with difficulty, but yet not so but that they can live, though they suffer some hardships. *Answer:* It don't answer the rules of Christian charity only to relieve those that are in extremity, as might be abundantly shown. . . .

When our neighbor is under difficulty he is afflicted; and we ought to have such a spirit of love to him that we should be afflicted with him in his affliction. And if we ought to be afflicted, then it will follow that we ought to be ready to relieve, because if we are afflicted with him, we relieve ourselves in relieving him; his relief is so far our relief as his affliction is our affliction. Christianity teaches us to be afflicted in our neighbor's affliction; and nature teaches us to relieve ourselves when afflicted. . . . That we should only relieve our neighbor when in extremity is not agreeable to that rule of loving our neighbor as ourselves.

Some may object against charity to a particular object, that he is an ill sort of person and has been injurious to them. He don't deserve that people should be kind to him; he is of a very ill temper; he is of an ungrateful spirit and is an ill sort of man upon other accounts; and, particularly, he had not deserved well of me, but has treated me ill, has been injurious, and has a spirit against me. *Answer:* We are obliged to relieve persons in want, notwithstanding those things, both by the general and particular rules of God's Word. . . . That which I particularly observe is that Christ here plainly teaches that our enemies, those that abuse and injure us, are our neighbors, and therefore come under the rule of loving our neighbor as ourselves.

Another general rule that obliges us to it is that wherein we are commanded to love one another as Christ has loved us; we have it in John 13:34, "A new commandment I give unto you, That ye love one another; as I have loved you, that ye also love one another." Christ calls it a new commandment with respect to that old commandment of the Lord, of loving our neighbor as ourselves. This, of loving our neighbor as Christ has loved us, implies something further in it than that. And 'tis, with respect to that, a new commandment, as it opens our duty to us in a new manner and in a further degree than that did. We must not only love our neighbor as ourselves, but as Christ hath loved us. . . .

Christ has loved us so as to be willing to deny himself and to suffer greatly for our help, so should we be willing to deny ourselves, and to suffer greatly to help others. Christ loved us, and showed us great kindness, though we were far below him; so should we be willing to love others, and show them kindness, though they be below us. Christ denied himself to help us, though we are not able to recompense him; so we should be willing to lay out ourselves to help our neighbor freely, expecting nothing again. . . .

Some may object from their own circumstances, that they have nothing to spare; they han't more than enough for themselves. To this, I say, *Answer:* That it must doubtless be allowed to be so in some cases that persons by reason of their own circumstances are not obliged to give to others. As, for instance, if there be a contribution for the poor, if those that are the poor themselves, are as much in need as those that the contribution is to be given to, it savors of a ridiculous pride and vanity in them to contribute with others, to give to those that are not more needy than they. It savors of a proud desire to conceal their own circumstances and an affection of having them accounted above what in truth they are. *But,* there is scarce anybody but what may make this objection, as they may mean by it. There is nobody but what may say he has not more than enough for himself, as he may mean by enough. . . .

Some may object, concerning a particular person, that they don't certainly know whether he be an object of charity or no. They ben't perfectly acquainted with his circumstances; they don't know whether he be in want, as he pretends, or, if he be, they don't know how he came to be in want, whether it was not by his own idleness, or whether he was not a spendthrift. They argue that they ben't obliged till they certainly know. . . .

Answer: 'Tis true, when we have opportunity to come to be certainly acquainted with their circumstances, 'tis well to improve it; and to be influenced in a measure by probability, in such cases is not to be condemned. But yet 'tis better to give to several that are not objects of charity, than to send away empty one that is. . . .

Some may say they ben't obliged to give to the poor till they ask: "If any man is in necessity, let him come and make known his straits to me, and it will be time enough for me to give then. Or if he needs a contribution let him come and ask; I don't know that the congregation or church are obliged to relieve persons till they ask relief." *Answer:* 'Tis surely most charitable to relieve the needy in that way wherein we shall do them the greatest kindness. Now 'tis certain that we shall do 'em a greater kindness by inquiring into their circumstances and relieving of 'em without putting of 'em upon begging. There is none of us all, but that if it were our case, we would look upon it so. We should think it more kind in our neighbors to inquire into our circumstances and help us of their own accord.

To be put upon begging in order to relief is, as the times are, a real difficulty; and we should, any of us, look upon it so. It is more charitable, more brotherly, more becoming Christians and the disciples of Jesus, to do it without. I think it is self-evident, and needs no proof. . . .

Objection: He [a poor person] has brought himself to want by his own fault. *Answer:* It must be considered what you mean by "his fault." If you mean a want of a natural faculty to manage affairs to advantage, that is to be considered as his calamity. Such a faculty is a gift that God bestows on some and not on others, and 'tis not owing to themselves. You ought to be thankful that God has given you such a gift that he has denied to him. . . .

If they are come to want by a vicious idleness or prodigality, yet we ben't thereby excused from all obligations to relieve 'em unless they continue in it. . . . If they continue in the same courses still, yet that don't excuse us from charity to their families that are innocent. If we can't relieve those of their families without them having something of it, yet that ought not to be a bar in the way of our charity; and that, because 'tis supposed that those of their families are proper objects of charity. And those that are so, we are bound to relieve; the command is positive and absolute. If we look upon that which the heads of the families have of it as entirely lost, yet we had better lose something of our estates than suffer those who are really proper objects of charity to remain without relief. . . .

The law makes provision for the poor and obliges the town to provide for them. And therefore some argue that there is no occasion for particular persons to exercise any charity this way. They say the case is not the same with us now as it was in the primitive church; for then Christians were under a heathen government. And therefore, however the charity of Christians in those times is much to commend, yet now, by reason of our different circumstances, there is no occasion for private charity. In the state that Christians are now in, provision is made for the poor otherwise.

This objection is built upon these two suppositions, both of which I suppose are false.

1. That the towns are obliged by law to relieve everyone that otherwise would be an object of charity. This, I suppose to be false, unless to be supposed that none are proper objects of charity but only those that have no estate left to live upon, which is very unreasonable, and what I have already shown the falseness of. . . .

Nor do I suppose it was ever the design of the law to cut off all occasion for Christian charity; nor is it fit there should be any such law. 'Tis fit the law should make provision for those that have no estates of their own; 'tis not fit that persons that are reduced to that extremity should be left to anything so precarious as a voluntary charity. They are in necessity of being relieved, and, therefore, 'tis fit that there should be something sure for 'em to depend upon. But a voluntary charity in this corrupt world is an uncertain thing; and therefore the wisdom of legislators did not think fit to leave those that are so reduced to such a precarious foundation for a subsistence. But I don't suppose it was ever the design of the law to make such a provision for all that are in want, as to leave no room for Christian charity. But then,

2. This objection is built upon another supposition that is equally false viz. that there are in fact none that are objects of charity but those that are relieved by the town. Let the design of the law be what it will, yet if there are in fact persons that are in want, so as to stand in need of our charity, notwithstanding that law, that don't free us from obligation to relieve 'em by our charity. For, as we have just now shown in answer to the last objection, if it more properly belongs to others to relieve them than we, yet if they don't do it, we ben't free. So that if that be true, that it belongs to the town to relieve all that are in want, so as otherwise to be proper objects of charity, yet if they in fact don't do it, we are not excused. If one of our neighbors suffers through the fault of a particular person, a thief or a robber, or of a town, it alters not the case; but if he

suffers and is without relief, 'tis an act of Christian charity in us to relieve him. Now, 'tis too obvious to be denied that there are in fact those that are in want, so that it would be a charitable act in us to help them, notwithstanding all that is done by the town as a town. A man must hide his eyes to think otherwise.

8

Sermon: "The Excellency of Christ" (1736)

Edwards preached "The Excellency of Christ" on a communion Sunday in the late summer of 1736. This special occasion, as was often the case with his social sermons, lent extra weight to the message, in this case what people in Northampton and Massachusetts might learn from what scripture reveals about Jesus Christ. This was a year or so after the Connecticut Valley Revival, a months-long local surge of intense piety, had faded. Edwards was seeking new ways to kindle holiness.

For Edwards, as for most New England ministers, Jesus Christ was the incarnation of God, the God-man who was fully human but also fully divine—the "King of Kings" who reigns so much higher than any worldly monarchs that they are mere dust by comparison. Yet Christ's true "excellency," according to Edwards, lay not in his greatness or glory but in his humility and "infinite condescension"—his willingness to stoop to the lowest levels of humanity.

Jesus, as Edwards detailed, walked on earth among beggars, slaves, children, and the despised, treating them all with remarkable grace and compassion. Moreover, Jesus was poor himself, a point Edwards had made more briefly in earlier sermons. Jesus was the son of a carpenter, was born to a woman so poor she had to sacrifice a dove instead of the customary lamb, and attracted fishermen and farmers as his followers. He lived his life in poverty, dwelling among the poor and surviving on charity. Although divinely supreme, he identified with the poor and outcast and surrounded them with his love.

Edwards thus fused two powerful images of Jesus—the Lion who saves by his strength and majesty, and the Lamb whose meekness and patience show the way to holy community. If Jesus condescended so meekly, so too surely should the local, provincial, and imperial well-to-do. Instead, said Edwards, deploying his special brand of invective, they exalt themselves like "worms on a dunghill," each struggling in a frenzy of status-seeking to be the greater worm.

From *The Works of Jonathan Edwards,* vol. 19, *Sermons and Discourses, 1734–1738,* ed. M. X. Lesser (New Haven: Yale University Press, 2001), 560–94.

DOCTRINE: There is an admirable conjunction of diverse excellencies in Jesus Christ.

There do meet in Jesus Christ, infinite highness, and infinite condescension. Christ, as he is God, is infinitely great and high above all. He is higher than the kings of the earth; for he is King of Kings, and Lord of Lords. He is higher than the heavens, and higher than the highest angels of heaven. So great is he, that all men, all kings and princes, are as worms of the dust before him, all nations are as the drop of the bucket. . . .

And yet he is one of infinite condescension. None are so low, or inferior, but Christ's condescension is sufficient to take a gracious notice of them. He condescends not only to the angel, humbling himself to behold the things that are done in heaven, but he also condescends to such poor creatures as men; and that not only so as to take notice of princes and great men, but of those that are of meanest rank and degree, "the poor of the world" (James 2:5). Such as are commonly despised by their fellow creatures, Christ don't despise. I Corinthians 1:28, "Base things of the worlds, and things that are despised, hath God chosen." Christ condescends to take notice of beggars and of servants, and people of the most despised nations: in Christ Jesus is neither "Barbarian, Scythian, bond, nor free" (Colossians 3:11). He that is thus high, condescends to take a gracious notice of little children. . . .

Such a conjunction of such infinite highness, and low condescension, in the same person, is admirable. We see by manifold instances, what a tendency an high station has in men, to make them to be of quite a contrary disposition. If one worm be a little exalted above another, by having more dust, or a bigger dunghill, how much does he make of himself! What a distance does he keep from those that are below him! And a little condescension, is what he expects should be made much of, and greatly acknowledged. Christ condescends to wash our feet; but how would great men (or rather the bigger worms), account themselves debased by acts of far less condescension!

There meet in Jesus Christ, infinite justice, and infinite grace. As Christ is a divine person he is infinitely holy and just, infinitely hating sin, and disposed to execute condign [fitting] punishment for sin. He is the Judge of the world, and the infinitely just judge of it, and will not at all acquit the wicked, or by any means clear the guilty.

And yet he is one that is infinitely gracious and merciful. Though his justice be so strict with respect to all sin, and every breach of the law, yet he has grace sufficient for every sinner, and even the chief of sinners. And it is not only sufficient for the most unworthy to show them mercy, and bestow some good upon them, but to bestow the greatest good; yea, 'tis sufficient to bestow all good upon them, and to do all things for them. . . .

In Jesus Christ, who is both God and man, these two diverse excellencies, are sweetly united. He is a person infinitely exalted in glory and dignity. . . . But however he is thus above all, yet he is lowest of all in humility. There never was so great an instance of this virtue, among either men or angels, as Jesus. None ever was so sensible of the distance between God and him, or had a heart so lowly before God, as the man Christ Jesus (Matthew 11:29). What a wonderful spirit of humility appeared in him, when he was here upon earth, in all his behavior! In his contentment in his mean outward condition, contentedly living in the family of Joseph the carpenter, and Mary his mother, for thirty years together, and afterwards choosing outward meanness poverty and contempt, rather than earthly greatness; in his washing his disciples' feet, and in all his speeches and deportment towards them; in his cheerfully sustaining the form of a servant through his whole life, and submitting to such immense humiliation at death! . . .

There are conjoined in the person of Christ, infinite worthiness of good, and the greatest patience under sufferings of evil. He was perfectly innocent, and deserved no suffering. He deserved nothing from God, by any guilt of his own; and he deserved no ill from men. Yea, he was not only harmless, and undeserving of suffering, but he was infinitely worthy, worthy of the infinite love of the Father, worthy of infinite and eternal happiness, and infinitely worthy of all possible esteem, love, and service from all men. And yet he was perfectly patient under the greatest sufferings. . . .

Having thus shown wherein there is an admirable conjunction of excellencies in Jesus Christ, I now proceed to show how this admirable conjunction of excellencies appears in Christ's acts. It appears in what Christ did in taking on him our nature. In this act his infinite condescension wonderfully appeared; that he that was God, should become man; that the Word should be made flesh, and should take on him a nature infinitely below his original nature! And it appears yet more remarkably, in the low circumstances of his incarnation: he was conceived in the womb of a poor young woman; whose poverty appeared in that when she came to offer sacrifices for her purification, she brought what was allowed of in the law, only in case of poverty; as Luke 2:24, "According to that which is said in the law of the Lord, a pair of turtledoves, or two young pigeons." This was allowed only in case the person was so poor, that she was not able to offer a lamb (Leviticus 12:8).

And though his infinite condescension thus appeared in the manner of his incarnation, yet his divine dignity also appeared in it; for though he was conceived in the womb of a poor virgin, yet he was there conceived by the power of the Holy Ghost. And his divine dignity also appeared in the holiness of his conception and birth. . . .

He was brought forth in a stable, because there was no room for them in the inn. The inn was taken up by others, that were looked upon as persons of greater account. The blessed Virgin being poor and despised, was turned or shut out; though she was in such necessitous circumstances, yet those that counted themselves her betters, would not give place to her; and therefore in the time of her travail she was forced to betake herself to a stable; and when the child was born, it was wrapped in swaddling clothes, and laid in a manger; and there Christ lay a little infant; and there he eminently appeared as a lamb. But yet this feeble infant that was born thus in a stable, and laid in a manger, was born to conquer and triumph over Satan. . . .

After he entered on his public ministry, his marvelous humility and meekness was manifested in his choosing to appear in such mean outward circumstances, and in being contented in them, when he was so poor that he had not where to lay his head, and depended on the charity of some of his followers for his subsistence; as appears by Luke 8, at the beginning. As also in his meek, condescending, and familiar treatment of his disciples; in the discourses with them, treating them as a father his children, yea, as friends and companions: and in his patient bearing such affliction and reproach, and so many injuries from the scribes and Pharisees, and others: in these things he appeared as a lamb. And yet he at the same time did in many ways show forth his divine majesty and glory; particularly in the miracles that he wrought, which were evidently divine works, and manifested omnipotent power, and so declared him to be the Lion of the tribe of Judah. . . .

Christ's humiliation was great, in being born in such a low condition, of a poor virgin, and in a stable: his humiliation was great, in being subject to Joseph the carpenter, and Mary his mother, and afterwards living in poverty, so as not to have where to lay his head, and in suffering such manifold and bitter reproaches as he suffered, while he went about preaching and working miracles: but his humiliation was never so great, as it was in his sufferings, beginning with his agony in the Garden, till he expired on the cross. . . .

Thus Christ appeared at the same time, and in the same act, as both a lion and a lamb. He appeared as a lamb in the hands of his cruel enemies; as a lamb in the paws, and between the devouring jaws of a roaring lion; yea, he was a lamb actually slain by this lion; and yet at the same time, as the Lion of the tribe of Judah, he conquers and triumphs over Satan, destroying his own devourer; as Samson did the lion that roared upon him, when he rent him as he would a kid. And in nothing has Christ appeared so much as a lion, in glorious strength destroying his enemies, as when he was brought as a lamb to the slaughter; in his greatest weakness, he was most strong; and when he suffered most from his enemies, he brought the greatest confusion on his enemies. . . .

And he still manifests his lamblike excellencies, in his dealings with his saints on earth, in admirable forbearance, love, gentleness, and compassions, instructing, supplying, supporting, and comforting them, often coming to them, and manifesting himself to them by his spirit, that he may sup with them, and they with him, admitting them to sweet communion with him, enabling them with boldness and confidence to come to him, and solace their hearts in him. And in heaven Christ still appears, as it were with the marks of his wounds upon him; and so appears as a lamb as it had been slain. . . .

This admirable conjunction of excellencies will be manifest in Christ's acts at the last Judgment. He then above all other times will appear as the Lion of the tribe of Judah, in infinite greatness and majesty, when he shall come in the glory of his Father, with all the holy angels, and the earth shall tremble before him, and the hills shall melt. . . .

And yet he will at the same time, appear as a lamb to his saints. He will receive them as friends and brethren, treating them with infinite mildness and love: there shall be nothing in him terrible to them; but towards them, he will clothe himself wholly with sweetness and endearment. The church shall then be admitted to him as his bride: that shall be her wedding day: the saints shall all be sweetly invited to come with him, to inherit the kingdom, and reign in it with him, to all eternity.

9

Sermon: "Charity Contrary to a Selfish Spirit" (1738)

In the early 1730s, Edwards started to deliver sermons that stretched over several preaching occasions. Later that decade, he began to deliver series of sermons, themselves sometimes in several parts, on the same topic over many consecutive weeks. Both these practices came from long Puritan tradition and fit Edwards's style of in-depth argument and analysis particularly well. "Charity Contrary to a Selfish Spirit" was part of *Charity and Its Fruits,* a twelve-sermon series delivered in mid-1738. His text for the series was I Corinthians 13.

Edwards was busy at the time promoting a town fund for the poor and probably preached the series partly to support this campaign. Unlike his 1733 sermon on the duty of charity (no. 7, above), where charity meant giving, here Edwards meant love in a broad sense because he wished to explore how love of God and love of other people could contain the baleful effects of love of self. This was a topic that increasingly preoccupied eighteenth-century thinkers, including ministers. It mattered to Edwards personally, in part because selfishness was a barrier to building holy community generally and a poor fund specifically.

Edwards's argument was simple: We must love God with all our hearts and minds as he has commanded. We will then devote ourselves to him, leaving less for self-love. We must also love other humans, whom God created in his image and as Christ taught. This includes even our enemies. We must look on them as ourselves and make their interests ours, thereby blending self-love with love to others. This will help us to realize that people possess worldly goods only through God's grace, and have neither absolute right nor liberty to improve them. They are for God and humanity.

Edwards's views stand in contrast to the individualism of Adam Smith's "invisible hand" or the moral sense theories of some other thinkers. Individualism for Edwards was at times a problem, not a solution. Instead, he seems almost to have urged the mystical sense of oneness with God and humanity that would follow upon an experience intense enough to transform a person's selfish heart—such as some would come to believe they had experienced during the Connecticut Valley Revival and the Great Awakening.

In this sermon, Edwards relied a little more than usual for one of his social sermons on biblical commands—scripture representing the highest pos-

From *The Works of Jonathan Edwards,* vol. 8, *Ethical Writings,* ed. Paul Ramsey (New Haven: Yale University Press, 1989), 252–71.

sible authority—rather than reason and experience. Also, he succeeded, as he preached here on love, in suppressing his habitually vigorous criticism of his parishioners.

Self-love is the sum of natural principles, as divine love is of supernatural principles. This divine love is no plant which grows naturally in such a soil as the heart of man. But it is a plant transplanted into the soul out of heaven; it is something divine, something from the holy and blessed Spirit of God, and so has its foundation in God, and not in self. And therefore there is no other love so much above a selfish principle as Christian love is, there is no love that is so free and disinterested. God is loved for himself and for his own sake; and men are loved not because of their relation to self, but because of their relation to God, either because they are the children of God, or because they have either the spiritual or natural image of God.

And therefore divine and Christian love above all love in the world, is contrary to a selfish spirit. Though other-love, a moral love, may in some respects be contrary to selfishness, as it may move men to a moral liberality and generosity, yet in other respects it agrees with a selfish spirit; because if we follow it up to its original, it arises from the same root, viz. a principle of self-love. But divine love has its spring elsewhere; its root is in Christ Jesus, and so is heavenly. It is not anything of this world, and it tends thither whence it comes. As it does not spring out of self, so neither does it tend to self. It delights in the honor and glory of God for his own safe, and not merely for their sakes. And it seeks and delights in the good of men for their sakes, and for God's sake. How Christian love is in a peculiar manner above and contrary to a selfish spirit appears by this, viz. it goes out even to enemies. There is that in the nature and tendency of it to go out to the unthankful and evil, and to those that injure and hate us, which is directly contrary to the tendency of a selfish principle, and quite above nature.

That Christian love is contrary to a selfish spirit will appear by a distinct consideration of what the Scripture teaches of the nature of love to God and love to men.

1. If we consider what we are taught of the nature of love to God, and particularly from this that the Scripture teaches that they who have true

love to God love him so as wholly to devote themselves to God. This we are taught in the sum of the Ten Commandments: "Thou shalt love the Lord thy God with all thy heart, and with all thy soul, and with all thy mind, and with all thy strength" (Mark 12:30). Here is contained in these words a description of a right love to God; and they teach us that they who love him aright do devote all to him, all their hearts, and all their souls, all their mind and all their strength, or all their powers and faculties. Surely, a man who gives all this wholly to God keeps nothing back, but devotes himself wholly and entirely to God. He who gives God all his heart, and all his soul, and all his mind, and all his power or strength, keeps nothing back; there is no room for any reserve. All who have true love to God have a spirit thus to do.

This shows how much a principle of true love to God is above a selfish principle. For if self be devoted wholly to God, then there is something above self which influences the man; there is something superior to self which takes self and makes an offering of it to God. A selfish principle never devotes self to another; the nature of it is to devote all others to self. They who have true love to God, love God as God, and as the supreme good; whereas the nature of selfishness is to set up self for God, to make an idol of self. That being which men respect as God, they devote all to. They who idolize self devote all to self, but they who love God devote all to him.

2. That Christian love is contrary to a selfish spirit will appear if we consider what the Scripture teaches us of the nature of Christian love to men. And there are two chief and most remarkable descriptions which the Scripture gives us of a truly gracious love to our neighbor, both of which show this.

(1) One is loving our neighbor as ourselves This we have in Leviticus 19–18, "Thou shalt not avenge, nor bear any grudge against the children of thy people, but thou shalt love thy neighbor as thyself." This Christ cites as the sum of all the duties of the second table of the [Mosaic] law in Matthew 22:39, "The second is like unto it, Thou shalt love thy neighbor as thyself." Now this is contrary to selfishness; for it is not of such a nature as confines the heart to self but leads it forth to others as well as self, and in like manner as it does to self it disposes persons to look on their neighbor as being, as it were, one with self, and not only to consider

our own circumstances and necessities, but to consider the wants of our neighbors as we do our own; not only to have regard to our own desires but to the desires of others, and to make their case our own, and to do to them as we would that they should do to us.

(2) Another remarkable description which the Scripture gives us of a gracious love to others, which shows how contrary it is to selfishness, is loving others as Christ hath loved us, as in John 13:34, "A new commandment I give unto you, That ye love one another; as I have loved you, that ye also love one another." . . .

Let us consider how this description which Christ gives of Christian love to others shows it to be contrary to selfishness, by considering in what manner Christ has expressed love to us, and how much there is in the example of his love to enforce the contrary of a selfish spirit. . . .

i. Christ set his love on those who were enemies to himself. There was not only no love to himself in those upon whom he set his love, but they were full of enmity, a principle of mortal hatred to him.

ii. Such was Christ's love to us that he was pleased in some respects to look on us as himself. By his love to men he has so espoused them and united his heart to them that he is pleased in many respects to look on them as himself. His elect were from all eternity dear to him, as the apple of his eye. He looked upon them so much as himself that he looked on their concerns as his concerns, their interest as his own, and has made their guilt his by a gracious assumption of it to himself, that it might be looked upon as his by divine imputation. And his love has sought to unite them so to himself as to make them, as it were, members of himself, so that they are his flesh and his bone. . . .

How far shall we be from a selfish spirit, and how contrary to it, if we love one another after such a manner, or if there be the like spirit of love in us towards others which was in Christ towards us. Our love to others will not depend on their love to us; but we shall do as Christ did to us, love them, though enemies. We shall not only seek our own things, but we shall be in our hearts so united to others that we shall look on their things as our own. We shall look on ourselves interested in their good, as it was in Christ towards us. We shall be ready to forego and part with our own things in many cases for the things of others, as Christ expended and was spent for us. And these things we shall do without any expectation of being requited by them, as Christ did such great things for us without expectation of any requital from us. . . .

The use which I would make of this doctrine may be to dissuade all from a selfish spirit and practice, and to exhort to seek that spirit which is contrary to it. Seek that by divine love your heart may be devoted to God, and to his glory, and to love your neighbor as yourself, as Christ has loved you; and do not look every one on his own things but everyone also on the things of others. And to stir you up to it, besides those things already mentioned, consider

First. You should not seek your own things only, for you are not your own. You have not made yourself, nor are you made for yourself; you are neither the author or end of your being. Nor is it you that uphold yourself in being, nor is it you that provides for yourself; you are not dependent on yourself. But there is another who hath made you, and preserves you, and provides for you. And he who has made you has made you for himself, and for the good of your fellow creatures, and not only for yourself. . . .

You must not henceforth treat yourself as your own, by seeking your own things only or chiefly. If you do so you will be guilty of robbing Christ. As you are not your own, so nothing which you have, is your own. Your abilities of body or mind, your outward possessions are, most of them, not your own. Neither have you any liberty to improve them, as if you had an absolute property in them, as you will do if you improve them only for your own private interest, and not for the honor of Christ, and for the good of others.

Second. If you seek the glory of God and the good of your fellow creatures, it is a sure way to have God seek your interest. . . .

If you are selfish, and make yourself and your own private interest your idol, God will leave you to yourself, and let you promote your own interest as well as you can. But if you do not seek your own but the things of Jesus Christ, the things of others, God will make your interest and happiness his charge; and he is infinitely more able to provide for it and to promote it than you are. So that not to seek your own, that is, not to seek your private worldly interest, is the best way of seeking your own in another sense. It is the most direct course you can take to obtain your truest happiness. When you are required not to be selfish you are not required, as has been already observed, not to love and seek our own happiness. You are required not mainly to seek your private and confined interest. But if you place your happiness in God, and in glorifying him and serving him by doing good, in this way, above all others, will you promote your own wealth, and your own honor and pleasure, and durable riches, and obtain a crown of glory, and pleasures forevermore.

10

Sermon: "Long-Suffering and Kindness" (1738)

Edwards preached "Long-Suffering and Kindness" as part of the *Charity and Its Fruits* series he delivered in mid-1738 on I Corinthians 13. The sermon reprised many of his earlier appeals for charity and social harmony, stressing in particular the importance of bearing injuries and insults without retaliating or harboring grudges. He devoted part of the sermon to explaining what injuries especially concerned him, beginning, as usual, with the kinds of economic damage—fraud, deception, oppressing the needy, refusing to settle debts or fulfill agreements—that people would be likely to perpetrate at all social levels of a trading town or province.

He also addressed other forms of injury at some length, mostly involving what later generations would call "hurting words": unfair criticism, false gossip, deliberate misrepresentations, uncharitable judging, open contempt. Taverns (Northampton and its environs had several) were one source of this kind of hurtful talk, but it also stemmed from the arrogance of authorities, the resentment of those under them, an unwillingness to compromise, and sheer negative attitudes. Hurting words, said Edwards, trigger a desire for revenge that prompts yet more desire for revenge and eventually a hatred that can last indefinitely. The use of "tongues as weapons" does lasting damage, making it all the harder to love one another as Christians should.

Respond instead, counseled Edwards, with meekness and humility in the spirit of Christ. Control your "inward" passions of ill will, remain serene, move the community closer to holy peace. Also, said Edwards, who was possibly his era's most acute student of human psychology, it will protect you from the psychic pain of a disturbed mind and a bitter heart.

"Long-Suffering and Kindness" contained familiar Edwardsean preaching devices—a string of objections and answers, for example, and illustrations from scripture, including, as was common with Edwards, Christ as an ethical model. The sermon relied heavily on appeals to parishioners' common sense and personal experience rather than on the judgment of God. It also acknowledged the value of civil law in protecting people from harm—tacit recognition that the words of ministers will not penetrate everyone.

From *The Works of Jonathan Edwards*, vol. 8, *Ethical Writings*, ed. Paul Ramsey (New Haven: Yale University Press, 1989), 185–217.

I would show how a Christian spirit disposes persons meekly to bear ill which is received from others, or the injuries which others do them. Meekness is a great part of the Christian spirit. Christ in that great call and invitation which we have in the close of the eleventh chapter of Matthew, where he calls all that labor and are heavy laden to come unto him, particularly mentions this as that in which he calls upon them who come to him to imitate him. "Learn of me, for I am meek and lowly in heart." And meekness, as it respects injuries received from men, is called long-suffering in Scripture, and is often mentioned as an exercise of the Christian spirit. Galatians 5:22, "But the fruit of the Spirit is love, joy, peace, long-suffering." . . . In speaking to this point, I would, first, briefly take notice of some of the various kinds of injuries which persons receive from others; second, what is meant by meekly bearing such injuries; third, how this love that is the sum of the Christian spirit will dispose men to do thus.

First. I would briefly take notice of some of the various kinds of injuries that persons suffer from others. Some injure others in their estates by unfairness in their dealings, by being fraudulent and deceitful with them, or at least leading them in the blind, and taking advantage of their necessities; or by unfaithfulness toward them, not fulfilling their promises and engagements, and being slack and slighty [careless] in any business in which they are employed by their neighbors, aiming at nothing but first to get their wages, not being careful to improve their time which they are hired to work for their neighbors; or by asking unreasonable prices for what they do; or by withholding what is due from their neighbor unjustly, neglecting to pay their debts, or unreasonably putting their neighbor to trouble and difficulty to get what is due from them.

There are many other ways in which men injure others in their dealings one with another. There is abundance of wicked and perverse ways which men have in their dealings, in which they are far from doing to others as they would that others should to them, and by which they provoke and irritate one another. Some injure others in their good name, by reproaching them, or speaking evil of them behind their backs. Abundance is done in this way. No injury is so common as this. The iniquity which is committed by men in all our taverns by what they say of one another behind their backs is beyond account. Some injure others by making or spreading false reports of others, and so slandering them.

And others, although what they say is not a direct falsehood, yet a great misrepresentation of things, represent things in their neighbors in the worst colors, and strain their faults, and set them forth beyond what they are, and speak of them in a very unfair manner.

A great deal of injury is done among neighbors by uncharitably judging one another, putting injurious constructions on one another's words and actions. Persons may greatly injure others in their thoughts by unjustly entertaining a mean opinion and low esteem of them. Some men are intolerably injurious to others in the contempt they have of them in their hearts, and also by a forwardness to think the worst of them. A great deal is done in injuring others in words. Men commonly make use of their tongues as their weapons. This therefore is represented as their "scourge," Job 5:21. And wicked men's tongues are in this respect compared to the tongues of some very poisonous kinds of serpents, whose weapon is their tongue, with which they mortally sting others. Psalms 140:3, "They have sharpened their tongues like a serpent; adders' poison is under their lips."

Sometimes men injure others in their behavior and actions towards them, or in the injurious deeds they do them. Sometimes persons who are vested with authority carry themselves very injuriously towards those over whom they have authority, by behaving themselves very injuriously and tyrannically towards them. And sometimes they who are under them that are in authority carry themselves very injuriously towards them, by denying them that respect and honor which is due to them in their places. Some carry themselves very injuriously towards others by the exercise of a very selfish spirit. Some men seem to be all for themselves, and in their carriage among men to have no regard to the good or benefit of their neighbor, but all their contrivance is to aggrandize themselves.

Some carry themselves as if they would set themselves above everybody, as though none was as good as they, and nobody was to be regarded but themselves. This appears in their talk and in their actions. When men carry themselves so, all who are about them, look upon themselves as injured by it, and very justly. Some carry themselves very injuriously by the exercise of a very willful spirit. Some are desperately set in their own way; they will, if possible, have things according to their wills, and never will alter or yield to others. They shut their eyes against light offered by others and will have no regard to anybody's inclinations but their own from a willful spirit. They are very perverse and unyielding in their ways. Some carry themselves very injuriously in the part they have in public affairs. What they do in such affairs is not so much from a regard to the public as from a spirit of opposition to a party, or to some particular person. By this the party or person opposed is injured, and oftentimes is greatly provoked and exasperated.

Some injure others by a spirit which they have against them. It is a common thing for neighbors to hate one another. They really have no love one to another in their hearts, but whether they own it or not do hate one another. They entertain in their breasts a spiteful disposition one towards another, by which they have no delight in each other's honor and prosperity they enjoy. Many injure others from a spirit of revenge. They will readily do things against others, remember some old thing, something which they have laid up against them. Some as long as they live entertain a grudge in their hearts against their neighbors. And commonly when it is so, there is not only one injury but a train and long series of injuries done towards them. And innumerable other particular ways of men's injuring one another might be mentioned, but these may suffice to suggest to us many of the most common of men's injuring one another. . . .

Second. What is meant by meekly bearing such injuries, or how they ought meekly to be borne. And here I would show, first, the nature of this virtue or duty; second, show why it is called long-suffering or suffering long.

1. I would show the nature of the duty of meekly bearing injuries in the following manner.

(1) It implies that injuries offered should be borne without doing anything to revenge them. When persons are going about to revenge an injury, then they no longer bear it. There are many ways in which men do that which is revengeful. Not only those things by which men do actually bring some immediate suffering on their neighbors, are revenge; but whatever men do either in speech or behavior against their neighbors, by which they vent any bitterness of spirit against their neighbors for injuries received. So if men after they are offended and injured speak reproachfully to their neighbor, or of him to others, with a design to make others think worse of him, to the end that they may gratify that

bitter spirit which they feel in themselves for the injury their neighbor has done them, that is revenge.

He, therefore, who exercises Christian long-suffering towards his neighbor bears injuries from him without revenging or retaliating, either with revengeful deeds or bitter words. He bears it without doing anything against his neighbor to gratify a bitter resentment, without talking with bitter words to him, without showing revengeful spirit in the manner of his countenance, or air of his behavior. He receives all with a calm, undisturbed countenance, still manifesting the quietness and goodness in this behavior towards him, both to his face and behind his back. . . .

(2) It implies that injuries be borne with the continuance of love in the heart; and without those inward motions and passions which tend to interrupt and destroy it. Injuries from our neighbors should be borne not only without manifesting an ill spirit outwardly in words or actions, but also without an ill spirit in the heart. We should not only lay violence on ourselves when we are injured, and refrain from giving vent to revenge, but the injury should be borne without revenge in the heart. Not only a smooth outward behavior should yet be continued, but also a sincere love. We should not cease to love our neighbor because he does us injury; we may pity him but not hate him for it.

(3) It implies that injuries be borne without losing the quietness and repose of our minds. They should not only be borne without a rough behavior, but with a continuance of inward calmness. When it comes to that, that injuries which are suffered disturb the calm of the mind and put it into a rustle and tumult, then it ceases to bear those injuries. As when a wind blows so strongly upon a house that the house ceases to remain still, and is much shaken and rocks, and begins to be moved from its foundation; this shows that the wind is higher than the house can bear. When men feel themselves much disquieted by injuries they receive, and their inward rest ceases, they cannot quietly enjoy themselves. They are so discomposed that they are not in a capacity well to attend the duties to which they are called; they cannot well compose their minds to prayer, or religious meditation. But their minds are diverted by the wrong they have received from their neighbor. This is something contrary to that long-suffering and meekly bearing injuries. . . . The minds of Christians ought still to have their calm and serenity maintained, whatever injuries they suffer. Their souls should be serene.

(4) It implies that, in many cases when we are injured, we be willing to suffer considerably in our own interest for the sake of peace rather than do what we have opportunity to do to defend ourselves. When men suffer injuries from others the case is often such that a Christian spirit, if men exercised such a spirit as they ought, would dispose to forbear to take the advantage they have to vindicate and redress themselves, *either because* if they do so, yet thereby they shall bring a very great calamity upon him who injures, and tenderness towards him may and ought to dispose to a great deal of forbearance, and to suffer something ourselves from him rather than to bring so great a suffering on him, though he injures us and so may in a sense be said to bring the suffering on himself; *or because* the consequence would probably be a violation of peace and an established alienation, whereas without it there may be hope of gaining our neighbor who unjustly uses us. These things are manifested from what the Apostle says to the Corinthians concerning going to law one with another. I Corinthians 6:7, "Now therefore there is utterly a fault among you, because ye go to law one with another." . . .

Not that all endeavors in men to defend and redress themselves when they are injured by their neighbor are unreasonable; or that men should suffer all injuries which their enemies please to bring upon them, rather than take an opportunity which they have in their hands to defend and vindicate themselves. . . .

Let what has been said under this doctrine be improved by us to suppress all wrath, revenge, and bitterness of spirit towards those who have injured, or may at any time injure us, whether they injure us in our estates or good names, and whether they abuse us with their tongues, or with their hands, and whether those who injure us are our superiors, inferiors or equals. Let us not say in our hearts, I will do to him as he hath done to me; let us not go about to strive to be even with him by any kind of retaliation, or so much as suffer any hatred or bitterness or disturbance of spirit to rise in our hearts. Let us seek that whatever injuries we receive the quiet and calm of our spirits may be continued, and let us be ready rather to suffer considerably in our just rights than to do that which may be an occasion of our stirring up and living in strife and contention. . . .

This world has ever been full of unreasonable men, men who will not be governed by rules of justice, but are carried on in that way in which their headstrong lusts drive them. When Christ was about to send his disciples out into the world, he told them, "I send you forth as sheep in the midst of wolves," Matthew 10:16. And therefore those who have not a spirit with meekness and calmness, and composedness of spirit to bear injuries in such a world are miserable indeed, and are like to be miserable; they are not at all fitted to live in and go through such a world as this is.

If every injury with which we meet, every reproach, every spiteful and unjust deed, must put our minds into a rustle and tumult, and disturb its calm and peace, that is the way never to enjoy ourselves or have the possession of ourselves, but to be kept in a perpetual turmoil and tumult like a bark that is continually driven to and fro on the stormy ocean. Men who have their spirits heated and enraged, and rising in bitter resentment when they are injured, or unreasonably dealt with, act as if they thought some strange thing had happened to them. Whereas they are very foolish in taking it so, it is no strange thing at all; it is no other than what is to be expected in such a world. Men therefore do not act wisely who have their spirits ruffled by injuries with which they meet. A wise man does not expect any other and is prepared for it, and composes his spirit to bear it. . . .

Persons' hearts are full of objections against such a meek and quiet bearing of injuries as has been spoken of, some of which I would briefly mention, and answer.

Objection. Some may be ready to say that the injuries they receive from men are intolerable; that as the other person has been so unreasonable in what he has said or done, it is so unjust and injurious and ungrateful and the like, that it is more than flesh and blood can bear. They are treated with so much injustice that it is enough to provoke a stone; or they are treated with such contempt that they are nearly trampled upon, and if you tread upon a worm it will turn. In answer to this I would ask the objector a few questions.

Question. Whether he thinks the injuries he has received are more intolerable than those which he has offered to God? whether they are more base, unreasonable, ungrateful, aggravated, and heinous; more in number or on any account whatsoever more provoking? . . .

Question. Did Christ turn again upon those who injured, and insulted, and trod on him when he was here below; and was he not injured far more grievously than ever you have been? Was not Jesus Christ trampled on and trod underfoot a thousand times more than ever you was? Did he turn again? Did you never tread underfoot the Son of God more than you was ever trodden? And is it a more provoking thing for men to tread on you than for you to tread on Christ?

Objection. My injurers will be encouraged to go on, and I shall expose myself to be injured more.

Answer. One end of civil government is to provide for the defense of men's just rights. . . .

Answer. When once such a method puts a stop to injuries, it has a contrary later effect. And in the observation and experience of men, it is generally found that a meek and long-suffering spirit puts an end to injuries, while a revengeful spirit does but provoke them. Romans 12:19–20, "Avenge not yourselves, but rather give place unto wrath: for it is written, Vengeance is mine; I will repay, saith the Lord. Therefore, if thine enemy hunger, feed him; if he thirst, give him drink: for in so doing thou shalt heap coals of fire on his head."

11

Sermon: "Heaven Is a World of Love" (1738)

"Heaven Is a World of Love" was the fifteenth and last of Edwards's great 1738 sermon series *Charity and Its Fruits.* Here he depicted the wonders of heavenly life with a rhetorical power and imaginative fertility easily comparable to his occasional but better-known evocations of the terrors of hell. Here he deployed some of his favorite images—sun, light, fountains, streams, gardens, planets, great trees, brilliant flames—and offered to his parishioners hope of God's boundless love as well as concern for God's judgment.

Heavenly love, said Edwards, flows perfectly and eternally from God through every heavenly being, from Christ to the saints to the angels. Some may dwell nearer to God—Edwards thought there would be ranks even in heaven—but these will be spiritual and mental gradations rather than differences of material wealth or worldly status. And because every saint will love all others completely, these heavenly ranks will not reduce anyone's happiness or provoke envy, contempt, or strife, unlike here on earth, where malignity and corruption breed pride and resentment in even the most gracious relationships.

Edwards's goal in this sermon was not merely to offer a picture of heaven. He also wanted, as usual, to offer a guide to living on earth. Therefore, he urged his congregation, strive to be as you aspire to be in heaven. Beat back jealousy, doubt, hypocrisy, and anxiety. Cast out fear. Prepare yourself. Labor to love one another. For if you ever arrive in heaven, it will be on the wings of faith and love.

TEXT. *Charity never faileth; but whether there be prophecies, they shall fail; whether there be tongues, they shall cease; whether there be knowledge, it shall vanish away. For we know in part, and we prophesy in part. But when that which is perfect is come, then that which is part shall be done away* (1 Corinthians 13:8–10).

Love resides and reigns in every heart here [in heaven]. The heart of God is the original seat or subject of it. Divine love is in him not as a subject

From *The Works of Jonathan Edwards,* vol. 8, *Ethical Writings,* ed. Paul Ramsey (New Haven: Yale University Press, 1989), 366–97.

which receives from another, but as its original seat, where it is of itself. Love is in God as light is in the sun, which does not shine by a reflected light as the moon and planets do; but by his own light, and as the fountain of light. And love flows out from him towards all the inhabitants of heaven. It flows out in the first place necessarily [freely] and infinitely towards his only begotten Son, being poured forth without measure, as to an object which is infinite, and so fully adequate to God's love in its fountain. Infinite love is infinitely exercised towards him.

The fountain does not only send forth large streams towards this object as it does to every other, but the very fountain itself wholly and altogether goes out towards him. And the Son of God is not only the infinite object of the Father's love, but he also infinitely loves the Father. The infinite essential love of God is, as it were, an infinite and eternal mutual holy energy between the Father and the Son, a pure, holy act whereby the Deity becomes nothing but an infinite and unchangeable act of love, which proceeds from both the Father and the Son. Thus divine love has its seat in the Deity as it is exercised within the Deity, or in God towards himself. . . .

And the saints and angels are secondarily the subjects of holy love. . . . As God has given the saints and angels love, so their love is chiefly exercised towards God, the fountain of it, as is most reasonable. They all love God with a supreme love. There is no enemy of God in heaven, but all love him as his children. They all are united with one mind to breathe forth their whole souls in love to their eternal Father, and to Jesus Christ, their common Head.

Christ loves all his saints in heaven. His love flows out to his whole church there, and to every individual member of it; and they all with one heart and one soul, without any schism in the body, love their common Redeemer. Every heart is wedded to this spiritual husband. All rejoice in him, the angels concurring. And the angels and saints all love one another. All that glorious society are sincerely united. There is no secret or open enemy among them; not one heart but is full of love, nor one person who is not beloved. As they are all lovely, so all see each other's loveliness with answerable delight and complacence [pleasure in acting virtuously]. Everyone there loves every other inhabitant of heaven whom he sees, and so he is mutually beloved by everyone. . . .

The love which is in the heart of God is perfect, with an absolute, infinite and divine perfection. The love of the angels and saints to God and Christ is perfect in its kind, or with such a perfection as is proper to their nature, perfect with a sinless perfection, and perfect in that it is commensurate with the capacities of their natures.

So it is said in the text, when that which is perfect is come, that which is in part shall be done away. Their love shall be without any remains of a contrary principle. Having no pride or selfishness to interrupt or hinder its exercises, their hearts shall be full of love. That which was in the heart as but a grain of mustard seed in this world shall there be as a great tree. The soul which only had a little spark of divine love in it in this world shall be, as it were, wholly turned into love; and be like the sun not having a spot in it, but being wholly a bright, ardent flame. There shall be no remaining enmity, distaste, coldness and deadness of heart towards God and Christ; not the least remainder of any principle of envy to be exercised towards any angels or saints who are superior in glory, no contempt and slight towards any who are inferior.

Those who have a lower station in glory than others suffer no diminution of their own happiness by seeing others above them in glory. On the contrary they rejoice in it. All that whole society rejoice in each other's happiness; for the love of benevolence is perfect in them. Everyone has not only a sincere but a perfect good will to every other. Sincere and strong love is greatly gratified and delighted in the prosperity of the beloved. And if the love be perfect, the greater the prosperity of the beloved is, the more is the lover pleased and delighted. For the prosperity of the beloved is, as it were, the food of love; and therefore the greater that prosperity is, the more richly is love feasted.

The love of benevolence is delighted in beholding the prosperity of another, as the love of complacence is delighted in viewing the beauty of another. So that the superior prosperity of those who are higher in glory is so far from being any damp to the happiness of saints of lower degree that is it an addition to it, or a part of it. There is undoubtedly an inconceivably pure, sweet and fervent love between the saints in glory; and their love is in proportion to the perfection and amiableness of the objects beloved. And therefore it must necessarily cause delight in them when they see others' happiness and glory to be in proportion to their amiableness, and so in proportion to their love of them.

Those who are highest in glory are those who are highest in holiness, and therefore are those who are most beloved by all the saints. For they love those most who are most holy, and so they will all rejoice in it that they are most happy. And it will be a damp to none of the saints to see them who have higher degrees of holiness and likeness to God to be more loved than themselves; for all shall have as much love as they desire, and as great manifestations of love as they can bear; all shall be fully satisfied.

The joy of heavenly love shall never be damped or interrupted by jealousy. Heavenly lovers will have no doubt of the love of each other. They shall have no fear that their professions and testimonies of love are hypocritical; they shall be perfectly satisfied of the sincerity and strength of each other's love, as much as if there were a window in all their breasts, that they could see each other's hearts.

There shall be no such thing as flattery or dissimulation in heaven, but there perfect sincerity shall reign through all. Everyone will be perfectly sincere, having really all that love which they profess. All their expressions of love shall come from the bottom of their hearts. The saints shall know that God loves them, and they shall not doubt of the greatness of his love; and they shall have no doubt of the love of all their fellow heavenly inhabitants. And they shall not be jealous of the constancy of each other's love. They shall have no suspicion that their former love is abated, that they have withdrawn their love in any degree from them for the sake of any rival, or by reason of anything in themselves which they suspect is disagreeable to them, or anything they have done which is disrelished, or through the inconstancy of their hearts. Nor will they in the least be afraid that their love towards them will ever be abated.

There shall be no such thing as inconstancy and unfaithfulness in heaven to molest and disturb the friendship of that blessed society. The saints shall have no fear that the love of God will ever abate towards them, or that Christ will not continue always to love them with the same immutable tenderness. And they shall have no jealousy one of another, for they shall know that by divine grace the love of all the saints is also unchangeable. . . .

[Let me] speak of the blessed fruits of this love, exercised and enjoyed in these circumstances. . . . [The first is] the most excellent and perfect behavior of the inhabitants of heaven towards God and one another. Divine love is the sum of all good principles, and therefore is the fountain whence

proceed all amiable actions. As this love will be perfect to the perfect ex-
clusion of all sin consisting in enmity against God and fellow creatures,
so the fruit of it will be a perfect behavior. Their life in heaven shall be
without the least sinful failure or error. They shall never turn to the right
hand or left in the least degree from the way of holiness. Every action shall
be perfect in all its circumstances. Every part of their behavior shall be
holy and divine in matter and form and end. We know not particularly
how the saints in heaven shall be employed; but in general we know they
are employed in praising and serving God. . . . And this they do perfectly,
being influenced by such a love as has been described. And we have reason to think that they are employed so as in some way to be subservient
[doing what others want] to each other's happiness under God; because
they are represented in Scripture as united together as one society, which
can be for no other purpose but mutual subserviency. And they are thus
mutually subservient by a most excellent and perfectly amiable behavior,
one towards another, as a fruit of their perfect love one to another. . . .

If heaven be such a world as we have heard, then this may lead us to
see a reason why contention has such an influence as it has to darken
persons' evidence of heaven. Experience teaches it to be so, in fact, when
principles of malignity and ill will prevail in God's people, as they are
liable to it through remains of corruption in their hearts, and they get
into a contentious frame, when they are engaged in any strife public or
private, and their spirits are engaged in opposition to their neighbors in
any affair, their former evidences for heaven seem to die away, and they
are in darkness about their state; they do not find that comfortable sat-
isfying hope which they used to enjoy.

So when converted persons get into ill frames in their families, the
consequence commonly, if not universally, is that they live without
much of a comfortable sense of heavenly things, or any lively hope of it.
They do not enjoy much of that spiritual calm and sweetness which others do who live in love and peace. They have not that help from God and
communion with him, and intercourse with heaven in their prayers, as
others have. The Apostle seems to speak of contention in families as having this influence. I Peter 3:7, "Likewise, ye husbands, dwell with them
according to knowledge, giving honor unto the wife, as unto the weaker
vessel, and as being heirs together of the grace of life; that our prayers be
not hindered." The Apostle here intimates that discord in families tends

to hinder Christians in their prayers. And what Christian is there, who has made the experiment, that has not done it to his sorrow; and whose experience will not witness to the truth of this? . . .

We all hope to have a part in heaven, that world of love of which we have heard, and that in a little time. Surely then we should endeavor to use the same temper of mind. Here let several things be considered as motives.

1. This is the way to be like the inhabitants of heaven. You have heard how they love one another; and therefore they, and they only, are conformed to them who live in love in this world. In this way you will be like them in excellence and loveliness, for their holiness and loveliness consists in being of such an excellent spirit. And this will be the way to make you like them in happiness and comfort. For this happiness and joy and rest lies in loving the inhabitants of that world. And by living in love in this world the saints partake of a like sort of inward peace and sweetness. It is this way that you are to have the foretastes of heavenly pleasures and delights.

2. This is the way to have a sense of the glory of heavenly things, as of God and Christ, and holiness, and heavenly enjoyments. A contrary spirit, a spirit of hatred and ill will greatly hinders a sense of those things. It darkens the mind and clouds such objects, and puts them out of sight. A frame of holy love to God and Christ, and a spirit of love and peace to men greatly disposes and fits the heart for a sense of the excellence and sweetness of heavenly objects it gives a relish of them. It, as it were, opens the windows by which the light of heaven shines in upon the soul.

3. This is the way to have clear evidences of a title to heaven. There are no evidences of a title to heaven but in feeling that which is heavenly in the heart. But by what has been said, it appears that heavenliness consists in love. Therefore the way to have clear evidences of a title is to live a life of love, and so seek the continual and lively exercises of such a spirit. You will find that this will cast out fear and give a strong hope of heaven, and be, as it were, an exercise of heaven in your hearts.

4. By living a life of love, you will be in the way to heaven. As heaven is a world of love, so the way to heaven is the way of love. This will best prepare you for heaven, and make you meet for an inheritance with the saints in that land of light and love. And if ever you arrive at heaven, faith and love must be the wings which must carry you there.

12

A History of the Work of Redemption: "The Millennium" (1739); *Miscellanies* Notebook: "The Millennium" (1740)

The prospect of a great millennial era (a time of heavenly peace and joy for roughly one thousand years) here on earth preoccupied Edwards as much in later life as it had in 1723. It might even have been more attractive to the Massachusetts thinker, given the remarkable if brief experience of holiness that had descended on the Connecticut River Valley in the mid-1730s. In the summer of 1739, he delivered the longest preaching series of his career, *A History of the Work of Redemption,* an account in thirty sermons of the ebb and flow of true religion from ancient times to the birth and death of Christ, the Christianization of the Roman Empire under Constantine, the history of the medieval and early modern church, and secular history through the Reformation until the eighteenth century. The end of the series forecasts the overthrow of the papist and Muslim Antichrists by Protestantism and the advent of the millennium prior to the Last Judgment.

In sermon 27 of *Work of Redemption,* Edwards tried to flesh out what life might be like in the golden age. There was still acknowledgment, as there had been in his youthful notes, of material prosperity and the same expectation of multiracialism. But multiracialism did not mean multiculturalism, and he placed far greater emphasis on uniformity of belief—on the triumph of evangelical Protestant religion, spread by means of the words of teachers and preachers, and with the life of the Spirit so permeating humanity that rich merchants would labor on behalf of holiness, rulers and ruled would love one another, and nations and empires would dwell in peace.

Unlike other utopians—Thomas More in the sixteenth century, for example, or Karl Marx in the nineteenth—Edwards did not believe this could last indefinitely. People were too fundamentally evil to dwell in love and harmony indefinitely, and anyway there would be too many of them. The perfect eternal society would arrive only in heaven. He nonetheless thought hard about how long the millennium might actually last. The second document here, from the *Miscella-*

From sermon 27 in *The Works of Jonathan Edwards,* vol. 9, *A History of the Work of Redemption,* ed. John F. Wilson (New Haven: Yale University Press, 1989), 471–86, and from Edwards's *Miscellanies* notebooks in *The Works of Jonathan Edwards,* vol. 20, *The "Miscellanies," 833–1152,* ed. Amy Plantinga Pauw (New Haven: Yale University Press, 2002), 50–52.

nies notebook of 1740, indicates his thinking about this on the cusp of the Great Awakening.

Two further points are worth noting. As with most of his contemporaries, Edwards thought the world was about six thousand years old. But he likewise knew that the Bible in such matters as time could not always be taken literally. It required interpretation to make sense. Also, to realize Edwards's vision would necessitate the spread of evangelical, Reformed Protestantism. While in his day Protestants were just beginning their worldwide missionary efforts, Catholics had already had much success in Asia and Latin America. Edwards and other Protestants were largely unaware of these successes.

A History of the Work of Redemption (1739)

TEXT. *For the moth shall eat them up like a garment, and the worm shall eat them like wool; but my righteousness shall be for ever, and my salvation from generation to generation.* (Isaiah 51:8)

There is a kind of a veil now cast over the bigger part of the world that keeps 'em in darkness; but then this veil shall be destroyed. . . . And then all countries and nations, even those that are now most ignorant, shall be full of light and knowledge. Great knowledge shall prevail everywhere. It may be hoped that many of the Negroes and Indians will be divines, and that excellent books will be published in Africa, in Ethiopia, in Turkey—and not only very learned men, but others that are more ordinary men, shall then be very knowing in religion. Isaiah 32:3–4, "The eyes of them that see shall not be dim, and the ears of them that hear shall hearken. The heart also of the rash shall understand knowledge." Knowledge then shall be very universal among all sorts of persons. . . .

There shall then be a wonderful unraveling the difficulties in the doctrines of religion, and clearing up seeming inconsistencies; "so crooked things shall be made straight, and rough places shall be made plain," and darkness shall become light before God's people. Difficulties in Scripture shall then be cleared up, and wonderful things shall be discovered in the word of God that were never discovered before. The great discovery of those things in religion that had been before kept hid seems to be compared to removing the veiling and discovering the ark of the testimony to the people that used to be kept in the secret of the temple and never seen by them. Thus at the sounding of the seventh angel, when 'tis proclaimed "that the kingdoms of this world are become the kingdoms of our Lord, and of his Christ," 'tis added that "the temple of God was opened in heaven, and there was seen in his temple the ark of his testament." So great shall be the increase of knowledge in this time that heaven shall be, as it were, opened to the church of God on earth.

It shall be a time of great holiness; now vital religion shall everywhere prevail and reign. Religion shall not be an empty profession as it now mostly is, but holiness of heart and life shall abundantly prevail. Those times shall be an exception from what Christ says of the ordinary state of the church, viz. that there shall be but few saved, for now holiness shall become general, Isaiah 60:21, "Thy people also shall be all righteous." Not that there will be none remaining in Christianless condition, but that visible wickedness shall be suppressed everywhere, and true holiness shall become general, though not universal. And it shall be a wonderful time, not only for the multitude of godly men, but for eminency of grace. . . .

And holiness shall then be, as it were, inscribed on everything, on all men's common business and employments, and the common utensils of life, all shall be as it were, dedicated to God and improved for holy purposes; everything shall then be done to the glory of God. . . . And so God's people then, as they shall be eminent for holiness of heart, so they shall also be for holiness of life and practice.

It shall be a time wherein religion shall in every respect be uppermost in the world. It shall be had in great esteem and honor. The saints have hitherto for the most part been kept under, and wicked men have governed; but now they will be uppermost. The kingdom "shall be given into the hands of the saints of the most High" God, Daniel 7:27.

They shall live and reign with Christ a thousand years, Rev. 20:4. In that day such persons shall be chiefly promoted. Vital religion then shall take the possession of kings' palaces and thrones, and those that are in highest advancement shall generally be holy men, Isaiah 49:23, "And kings shall be thy nursing fathers, and their queens thy nursing mothers." Kings shall then improve all their power and glory and riches for the advancement of the honor and glory of Christ and the good of his church, Is. 60:16, "Thou shalt also suck the milk of the Gentiles, and shalt suck the breasts of kings." And the great men of the world, the rich merchants and others that have great wealth and influence, shall devote all to Christ and his church, Ps. 45:12, "The daughter of Tyre shall be there with a gift; . . . the rich among the people shall intreat thy favor."

These will be times of great peace and love. There shall then be universal peace and good understanding among all the nations of the world, instead of such confusion, war, and bloodshed as has hitherto been from one age to another, Isaiah 2:4. . . .

And then shall malice and envy and wrath and revenge be suppressed everywhere, and peace and love shall prevail between one man and another. Which is most elegantly set forth in the eleventh chapter of Isaiah, verses six through nine, "The wolf also shall dwell with the lamb. . . ." Then shall there be peace and love between rulers and ruled. Rulers shall love their people, and with all their might seek their best good; and the people shall love their rulers, and shall joyfully submit to them, and give 'em that honor that is their due. And so shall there be an happy love and peace everywhere between ministers and people. . . .

Then shall flourish in an eminent manner those Christian virtues of meekness, forgiveness, long-suffering, gentleness, goodness, brotherly kindness, those excellent fruits of the Spirit. Men in their temper and disposition shall then be like the lamb of God, the lovely Jesus. The body shall be conformed to the head.

And then shall all the world be united in peace and love in one amiable society; all nations, in all parts, on every side of the globe, shall then be knit together in sweet harmony, all parts of God's church assisting and promoting the knowledge and spiritual good one of another. A communication shall be then upheld between all parts of the world to that end, and the art of navigation that is now improved so much in fear, with covetousness and pride, and is used so much by wicked, debauched men, shall then be consecrated to God, and improved for holy uses. . . . And it shall then be a time wherein men will be abundant in expressing their love one to another, not only in words but in deeds of charity, as we learn, Isaiah 32:5, and "the vile person shall no more be called liberal, nor the churl be said to be bountiful." . . .

A time of excellent order in the church discipline and government shall be settled in his church; all the world shall then be as one church, one orderly, regular, beautiful society, one body, all the members in beautiful proportion. Then shall that be verified in Psalms 122:3, "Jerusalem is builded as a city compact together."

The church of God shall be beautiful and glorious on these accounts, yea it will appear in perfection of beauty. . . . As a bride adorned for her husband, the church will then be the greatest image of heaven. That will be a time of great temporal prosperity. Such a spiritual state will have a natural tendency to it: to health, Zechariah 8:4; ease, quietness, pleasantness, wealth, great increase of children, Zechariah 8:5. Through the remarkable blessing of heaven, Isaiah 65:21, "They shall build houses, and inhabit them; and they shall plant vineyards, and eat the fruit of them." . . .

I will speak briefly of the duration of the prosperous state of the church. It will be a long time, Revelation 20:4, "And I saw the souls of them that were beheaded for the witness of Jesus . . . and they lived and reigned with Christ a thousand years"; Isaiah 60:15, "Whereas thou hast been forsaken and hated, so that no man went through thee, I will make thee an eternal excellency, a joy of many generations."

Miscellanies: Entry 836 (1740)

When the duration of the glorious times of the church on earth after the fall of Antichrist (the Pope) is spoken of in the 20th chapter of Revelation as being a thousand years, the words are to be literally understood that it will be about that space of time, though perhaps it will not be so precisely; and if it be so precisely, it will probably be difficult precisely to fix the beginning, and so the end of it. Because, if the thousand years in chapter 20 of Revelation is not to be understood literally but figuratively, then 'tis probable that a vastly longer space of time is intended than a literal thousand years. For the manner of Scripture prophecy is to represent the true time by other times that are vastly less; thus a prophetical day is a year, a prophetical year 360 years. And if this thousand years here be used as a figurative and prophetical thousand years, it probably is to represent a vastly long space of time, as a thousand years seems to men to be a great while. Thus a day, an hour and a moment seem to men to be very short spaces of time; hence they are used to represent any short space of time as the shortness of man's life, etc. But the following reasons induce me to think that the space here meant is not any space of time vastly longer than a thousand years:

1. 'Tis not likely that the face of the earth would hold the inhabitants for a vastly longer time than a thousand years, multiplying so fast as they will under such great universal and uninterrupted prosperity, health and long life, which the generations of men shall enjoy throughout that space of time, without being diminished with wars, pestilences and other desolating calamities which now waste mankind. If we should suppose that at the beginning of the glorious times there should be just the same number of inhabitants on the face of the earth as now, and that their number should be doubled but once in a hundred years, which is the least that may be supposed under such prosperity; then at the end of one thousand years, there will be about a thousand times so many inhabitants on the earth as now there is. And at the end of two thousand years there must be a million times so many, and at the end of three thousand years a million million times so many inhabitants, as are now on the face of the earth.

2. That the world should continue standing such a vastly long time that a thousand years should be but a figure, or type, of the time, hardly consists with what the Scripture says of the near approach of the day of judgment.

13

Sermon: "Mercy and Not Sacrifice" (1740)

Edwards preached "Mercy and Not Sacrifice" in early 1740. This was shortly after the young revivalist George Whitefield arrived in America and began preaching to large crowds, and shortly before Whitefield came to Northampton to meet Edwards and preach to the valley communities. This sermon was sharply critical of rote external worship, and Edwards may have intended it as a step toward the kind of fervor Whitefield was stirring. But since it so forcefully privileged works of caring over external duties, it might also have reflected his frustration that the town had not yet responded to his call for a poor fund (which was established two years later).

Edwards acknowledged in this sermon that what he called the "internal" worship of God, by which he meant loving God with all our hearts and minds, is the essence of all faith. But he also argued that acts of mercy, justice, righteousness, and charity mattered more than "wooden" acts of public prayer, attendance at meetings, visible tithing, verbal professions of faith, and sacramental devotions. As evidence he offered God's commandment to love our neighbors, Christ's instruction to "love one another," and passages from James and Timothy disparaging the Pharisees' "self-righteous" addiction to form over substance.

Mercy, according to Edwards, is a logical extension of faith. God is infinitely powerful and does not need formal worship, only internal devotion. People, God's creations in his own image, are by contrast weak and therefore need charity. And since deeds of mercy involve self-denial, they are part of the unending Christian struggle against pride, envy, greed, and sensuality. Because they are denials of the self, they are more pleasing to God.

Edwards also argued that acts of charity, even if they are not actually rooted in faith, are good in themselves because they help people and thus adhere to the common moral law. Moreover, he reiterated, no one can survive alone, so that helping others helps to sustain the human race. Both these arguments represented not only biblical themes but also Enlightenment thinking, which was as important a feature of eighteenth-century culture as evangelicalism, and one in which Edwards would prove thoroughly adept.

From *The Works of Jonathan Edwards*, vol. 22, *Sermons and Discourses, 1739–1742*, ed. Harry S. Stout and Nathan O. Hatch (New Haven: Yale University Press, 2003), 111–35.

DOCTRINE: *Moral duties towards men are a more important and essential part of religion than external acts of worship of God.*

Moral duties towards men are not more essential parts of religion than acts of the internal worship of God. It must be observed that what is asserted in the doctrine, is that they are more essential or important than external or outward acts of worship, not the internal. The internal acts of worship, or the worship of the heart in inward acts of love and fear of God and trust in God, are the most essential and important of all the duties of religion whatsoever. Christ teaches us this; he tells us that the first and great command of the Law is to love the Lord our God with all our heart, and with all our soul, and with all our mind (Matthew 22:37–38). This is the very essence of all true religion, the most fundamental part, the source.

But moral duties towards men—such as being chaste and temperate and meek in our behavior, observing trust between man and man, showing mercy to others when acts of mercy towards 'em are required, and living honestly and charitably, and behaving ourselves humbly and contentedly amongst men, avoiding contempt among or coveting what is our neighbor's—such duties as these are of greater importance in religion than going to public or private meetings, attending outward acts of prayer or the ordinances of worship. For though no duty is to be made light of—no one is to be neglected; when we do some we ought not to leave others undone, but our obedience should be universal; and he that offends on one point is guilty of all; and every sin as committed against God deserves death eternal—and though neither one duty nor the other is of any value in the sight of God unless performed in sincerity, yet that don't hinder but that there are some matters that are weightier matters of the law than others, as most certainly there are by Christ's own testimony in the twenty-third chapter of Matthew, v. 23. There are three things that are there mentioned as weightier matters of the law: judgment, mercy and faith. The two first are moral duties towards men, viz. judgment and mercy, or, in other words, acts of justice and charity. . . .

Moral duties towards men are much more insisted on, both in the Old Testament and New, than the other. 'Tis true both are required; but the former are abundantly more insisted on in the Word of God. They are so in the Old Testament, when the church was under a dispensation wherein the externals of worship were much more insisted on, than under the New Testament, which is a dispensation of the Spirit and wherein especially men are called upon to worship God in the Spirit. Yet even under that old legal dispensation, how much more did the prophets insist on moral duties towards men, such as walking uprightly, working righteousness, speaking the truth every man to his neighbor, despising the gain of oppressions, shaking their hands from holding of bribes, stopping their ears from hearing of blood, seeking peace and ensuring it, executing true judgment, showing mercy and compassion every one to his brother, not oppressing the widow nor the fatherless nor the stranger nor the poor, not imagining evil against their brother in their hearts. . . .

And when we look into the writings of the apostles, external acts of worship are indeed in some places mentioned and required, but they are in no measure insisted on as moral duties towards men are. As in the epistles of the apostle Paul particularly, 'tis observable that the Apostle in his epistles commonly observes this method: that in the former part of his epistles he insists on doctrinal matter, but in the latter part he comes to what more immediately relates to practice and the duties that are required of Christians.

And there we may find that he insists ten times so much on moral duties towards men as the external acts of worship. . . .

Sometimes a professing people abound in acts of external worship when 'tis a very corrupt time among them, but not in duties of righteousness and charity towards their neighbors. . . .

Hypocrites and self-righteous persons do much more commonly abound in the outward acts of worship of God than they do in the duties of righteousness and mercy towards their neighbors. Thus it was with those notorious, self-righteous hypocrites in Christ's time, viz. the Pharisees. They very greatly abounded in the external acts of worship, such as prayers and fasting, and reading and teaching the law, and making proselytes, and tithing mint and anise and cumin, seemed to spend almost all their time in acts of worship of God, so that the people had an extraordinary opinion of their holiness; but yet were notoriously negligent of acts of righteousness and mercy. . . .

'Tis evident that duties of righteousness and charity are a more important and essential part of religion than external acts of worship of God, because when the Scriptures direct us to show our faith by our works, it is principally the former that are intended. The apostle James says, in James 2:18, "Yes, a man may say, Thou hast faith, and I have works: show me thy faith without thy works, and I will show thee my faith by my works." And it is there works of mercy and Christian behavior towards men that he chiefly means, as appears by all the context. For he had before been insisting on this kind of works only, as in the last verse of the foregoing chapter: "Pure religion and undefiled before God and the Father is this, To visit the fatherless and widows in their affliction, and to keep himself unspotted from the world." . . .

External worship is of no use but only as a sign of something else, viz. a sign of internal worship. But doing deeds of justice and charity is the very matter of moral righteousness. God says in the first chapter of Isaiah, v. 12, "When ye come to appear before me, who hath required this at your hand"? I.e. "I have never required this for its own sake; your appearing before me is of no use for itself, but only as a sign of something else."

Bowing or kneeling before God in men is of no more use, unless as a sign of inward reverence, than the same postures would be in a wooden statue. And so of other external expressions of worship. But doing deeds of justice and mercy towards men is in itself the very matter of moral righteousness. Indeed, they may want the right form, as they may want sincerity, but the deed themselves are the matter of moral righteousness. When a man does an act of justice, though if it ben't done in sincerity 'tis not acceptable to God, it is of some use and significancy in itself, because thereby right takes place. So when a man deals truly and faithfully.

When a man does an act of mercy, it is of significance in itself, for it is to do good. The act carries that in its own nature, viz. doing good. . . .

To show respect to God in acts of righteousness and mercy towards men is more to the honor of God than performing the external act of worship, because there is greater self-denial in it. It is a way of showing respect to God that is much more contrary to men's lusts [worldly obsessions]. Indeed, men's lusts are contrary to all religion; their sloth and their enmity against God tends to make 'em opposed to outward acts of worship. . . .

But men's lusts are much more contrary to the other kind of duties. A man may be strict in coming to meeting, and attending ordinances, and with his mouth showing much love, and yet all the while live in the most gross indulgence of all manner of lusts. Men's lusts will bear ten times as well with those outward forms of worship as with strictness of life in their behavior towards themselves and their neighbors, as the Pharisees and many other such hypocrites found. If you will let wicked men enjoy their covetousness and their pride, and their malice and envy, and their revenge and their sensuality and voluptuousness in their behavior among men, they will be content to put on a religious face in the meeting house or at private religious meetings and will submit to what forms of worship you please, and as many as you will. . . .

Therefore, it being so that those moral duties towards men are so much more contrary to men's lusts than external acts of worship, they must be more to God's honor, because there is greater self-denial in them. He that denies himself most for God, honors God most. And the duties must be of greatest importance.

As God is more honored, so more good is done to men by the performance of those duties than the other. For that is the nature of those acts: they materially consist in doing good to mankind. To show mercy to men is to do good to men, and to do acts of justice to men, we do good to mankind. Hereby we avoid doing others wrong, or doing injuries to them. So that both the great ends of religion are more answered by this sort of duties than the other. . . .

Hereby also is more good done to men's bodies. Justice and charity are the great things by which the good of human society are maintained and promoted, and love to God and love to men both are expressed in them. As to external acts of worship, or "bodily exercise," as the Apostle calls it, it profits little (I Timothy 4:8). It can't be profitable to God, nor is pleasing to him otherwise than as a sign and expression of internal worship, nor does so much tend to the profit of men.

Seeing, therefore, more good is done by those moral duties, they are of greater importance, are more acceptable to God, as they are more agreeable to the merciful nature of God. What God seeks in the commands he give us is our good and advantage, and not his own, for he is infinitely above any need of anything that we can do. . . .

This may teach us how we may best judge of the state of religion in a town. It looks well when there is a great deal of religious discourse in a town, at least if it be managed prudently and without any show of ostentation. It looks well if there be a great deal done at outward acts of worship. It looks well if a people are forward to come to the public worship, show a spirit to come seasonably to meeting and carry themselves devoutly in times of pubic worship. It looks well if a people are forward to embrace opportunities of outward worship, of going to private meetings. Such things look very well and gives ground to hope that there is a great deal of religion among a people.

But it looks yet a great deal better when a professing people do excel other people in a just and righteous, humble, meek, peaceable, quiet, loving conversation one among another, far from all revenge and ill will, all living in love, studying to promote one another's good, abounding in deeds of righteousness and mercy, apt to forbear with one another, apt to forgive one another, ready to deny themselves one for another, living together like a society of brethren in all Christian and holy behavior one towards another.

14

"A Church Covenant" (1742)

From 1740 to 1742, Northampton experienced a resurgence of the spiritual flowering that swept the immediate area in the mid-1730s, one part of an inter-colonial religious revival powerful enough to be called by historians "The Great Awakening." Edwards played a significant, if local, role in fomenting the Great Awakening. But he had seen the fervor of the 1730s revival dissipate quickly, was beginning to doubt revivalism's staying power, and searched for ways to sustain the piety and good behavior it generated.

One way he hit on was a written "covenant" for townspeople to endorse. In early Puritan days, covenant renewals—swearing in public to live Christian lives in exchange for God's blessing—were fairly common. They were not, however, common by the mid-eighteenth century, and almost never in written form. Edwards drafted this covenant himself, then built support for it by showing it to "principal men" in the congregation, to neighborhood groups, and to the whole congregation in public. Everyone above age fourteen signed the covenant and signaled their consent by standing in the meeting house on a day of fasting and prayer.

The document reprised standard Edwardsean themes: fair and honest economic dealings; no slandering, backbiting, or bearing grudges; managing public affairs through compromise and for the general welfare; not falling prey in youth to irreligion or lasciviousness; laboring diligently on behalf of religion. Most if not all of this could easily be found in fifteen years of sermons.

A few other points deserve mention. The covenant began predictably with economic matters but included an unusual paragraph binding anyone who injured someone financially to pay restitution. This would have been a big challenge in a trading community such as Northampton and particularly in New England's maritime centers where the awakening also flourished. Some surely signed only reluctantly. Townspeople swore not to tolerate enmity and ill will, especially over property and privileges, or to allow the forming of "parties," which Edwards detested as much as George Washington and John Adams would. The covenant also promised the "watchful" performance of (unspecified) family duties and, curiously, forswore "sloth," which Edwards seldom mentioned. Awakening fervor soon faded anyway.

From *The Works of Jonathan Edwards*, vol. 4, *The Great Awakening*, ed. C. C. Goen (New Haven: Yale University Press, 1972), 550–54.

Acknowledging God's great goodness to us, a sinful, unworthy people, in the blessed manifestations and fruits of his gracious presence in this town, both formerly and lately, and particularly in the very late spiritual revival; and adoring the glorious majesty, power, and grace of God, manifested in the present wonderful outpouring of his Spirit, in many parts of this land, in this place; . . . we do this day present ourselves before the Lord, to renounce our evil ways, we put away our abominations from before God's eyes, and with one accord to renew our engagements to seek and serve God: and particularly do now solemnly promise and vow to the Lord as follows:

In all our conversation, concerns, and dealings with our neighbor, we will have a strict regard to rules of honesty, justice, and uprightness, that we don't overreach or defraud our neighbor in any matter, and either willfully, or through want of care, injure him in any of his honest possessions or rights, and in all our communication will have a tender respect, not only to our own interest, but also to the interest of our neighbor; and will carefully endeavor, in every thing, to do to others as we should expect, or think reasonable, that they should do to us, if we were in their case, and they in ours.

And particularly we will endeavor to render every one his due, and will take heed to ourselves, that we don't injure our neighbor, and give him just cause of offense, by willfully or negligently forbearing to pay our honest debts.

And wherein any of us, upon strict examination of our past behavior, may be conscious to ourselves, that we have by any means wronged any of our neighbors in their outward estate, we will not rest, till we have made that restitution, or given that satisfaction, which the rules of moral equity require; or if we are, on strict and impartial search, conscious to ourselves that we have in any other respect considerably injured our neighbor, we will truly endeavor to do that which we in our consciences suppose Christian rules require, in order to a reparation of the injury, and removing the offense given thereby.

And furthermore we promise that we will not allow ourselves in back-biting; and that we will take great heed to ourselves to avoid all violations of those Christian rules, . . . and that we will not only not slander our neighbor, but also will not feed a spirit of bitterness, ill will, or secret grudge against our neighbor, insist on his real faults needlessly, and when not called to it, or from such a spirit, speak of his failings and blemishes with ridicule, or an air of contempt.

And we promise that we will be very careful to avoid doing anything to our neighbor from a spirit of revenge. And that we will take great care that we do not, for private interest or our own honor, or to maintain ourselves against those of a contrary party, or to get our wills, or to promote any design in opposition to others, do those things which we on the most impartial consideration are capable of, can think in our consciences will tend to wound religion, and the interests of Christ's kingdom.

And particularly, that so far as any of us, by Divine Providence, have any special influence upon others, to lead them in the management of public affairs, we will not make our own worldly gain, or honor, or interest in the affections of others, or getting the better of any of a contrary party, that are in any respect our competitors, or the bringing or keeping them down, our governing aim, to the prejudice of the interest of religion, and the honor of Christ.

And in the management of any public affair, wherever there is a difference of opinions, concerning any outward possessions, privileges, rights, or properties, we will not willingly violate justice for private interest: and with the great strictness and watchfulness will avoid all unchristian bitterness, vehemence, and heat of spirit; yea, though we should think ourselves injured by a contrary party; and in the time of the management of such affairs will especially watch over ourselves, our spirits, and our tongues, to avoid all unchristian inveighings, reproachings, bitter reflectings, judging and ridiculing others, either in public meetings or in private conversation, either to men's faces, or behind their backs; but will greatly endeavor with Christian humility, gentleness, quietness, and love.

And furthermore we promise that we will not tolerate the exercise of enmity and ill will, or revenge in our hearts against any of our neighbors; and we will often be strictly searching and examining our own hearts with respect to that matter.

And if any of us find that we have an old secret grudge against any of our neighbors, we will not gratify it but cross it, and endeavor to our utmost to root it out, crying to God for his help; and that we will make it our true and faithful endeavor, in our places, that a party spirit, may not be kept up amongst us, but that it may utterly cease; that for the future, we may all be one, united in undisturbed peace and unfeigned love.

And those of us that are in youth do promise never to allow ourselves in any diversions or pastimes, in meetings, or companies of young people, that we, in our consciences, upon sober consideration, judge not well to consist with, or would sinfully tend to hinder, the devoutest and most engaged spirit in religion, or indispose the mind for that devout and profitable attendance on the duties of the closet, which is most agreeable to God's will, or that we, in our most impartial judgment, can think tends to rob God of that honor which he expects, by our orderly serious attendance on family worship.

And furthermore we promise that we will strictly avoid all freedoms and familiarities in company, so tending either to stir up or gratify a lust of lasciviousness that we cannot in our consciences think will be approved by the infinitely pure and holy eye of God, or that we can think, on serious and impartial consideration, we should be afraid to practice, if we expected in a few hours to appear before that holy God, to give an account of ourselves to him, as fearing they would be condemned by him as unlawful and impure.

We also promise with great watchfulness to perform relative duties required by Christian rules, in the families we belong to, as we stand related respectively, towards parents and children, husbands and wives, brothers and sisters, masters or mistresses, and servants.

And we now appear before God, depending on divine grace and assistance, solemnly to devote our whole lives, to be laboriously spent in the business of religion; ever making it our greatest business, without backsliding from such a way of living, nor hearkening to the solicitations of our sloth. . . .

And being sensible of our weakness and the deceitfulness of our own hearts, and our proneness to forget our most solemn vows and lose our resolutions we promise to be often strictly examining ourselves by these promises, especially before the sacrament of the Lord's Supper; and beg of God that he would, for Christ's sake, keep us from wickedly dissembling in these our solemn vows; and that he who searches our hearts, and ponders the path of our feet, would, from time to time, help us in trying ourselves by this covenant, and help us to keep covenant with him, and not leave us to our own foolish, wicked and treacherous hearts.

15

Sermon: "The Duties of Christians in a Time of War" (1745)

Edwards preached this sermon in April 1745 shortly after the Americans joined the British in a conflict with France that centered in Europe but reached into the Western Hemisphere and Asia. King George's War, as the Americans called it, was only one of several Franco-British conflicts to touch the North Americans. In the first, fought when Edwards was a still a child, his father served briefly as a militia chaplain. Edwards, as his earlier sermons make clear, thought of defense as one of colonial leaders' main responsibilities.

But it was not one to be undertaken lightly. Christ, at least as Edwards depicted him, was the embodiment of humility and forgiveness. God's sixth commandment forbade "killing," but Edwards and most of the Christian tradition, following the sense of the Hebrew text, interpreted this as forbidding unjustified killing such as murder. Edwards believed this commandment in fact required self-defense and the "vigorous" prosecution of a just war. Colonial officials proposed not merely to defend New England against French attack but to send 4,300 troops (20 of them from Northampton) against a French citadel on Cape Breton Island in Canada, an operation that Edwards apparently thought was the sort of vigorous operation that would forestall future French attacks. But he also worried that it would involve both huge expenditures and much death and sorrow.

"Duties in a Time of War" addressed these and other important matters. Many of Edwards's arguments relied on notions of just war and the right of self-preservation that were commonplace among serious Western thinkers, including ministers and clerics. He pointed out that self-preservation meant preserving rights and privileges—to elected assemblies, presumably, or religious autonomy, neither of which would survive conquest by a France that was Catholic and, therefore, it was assumed, absolutist. Other points involved the strategy and tactics of this particular war—the ongoing Franco-British struggle; the danger Cape Breton posed to colonial fishing and coastal security; whether France, Europe's greatest land power, might conquer new areas of North America.

Edwards acknowledged that people could reasonably refuse to support a war they considered unjust. He clearly thought this one was just, in part because, like

From *The Works of Jonathan Edwards*, vol. 25, *Sermons and Discourses, 1743–1758*, ed. Wilson H. Kimnach (New Haven: Yale University Press, 2006), 127–41.

most New Englanders, he saw it as a phase in the great struggle between Protestants and Catholics. He thought for this reason that God would probably favor Britain—but only if people prayed ardently for that favor. When the expedition succeeded against all odds and the fortress fell, he felt understandably validated.

Proposition I. A people of God may be called of God to go forth to war against their enemies. This will appear by the consideration of these two things:

First. It is lawful and a duty in some cases for one nation to wage war with another. Reason and the light of nature shows it; it follows from the law of self-preservation. If it be lawful for a particular person, to stand in his own defense and to wound and kill another to preserve his own life, the very same principles that prove the lawfulness of one will prove the other. If it be lawful for a particular person to defend him with force, then it is lawful for a nation or people. A nation is made up of particular persons, and when particular persons are endangered, they can't be defended without the efforts of others. What is lawful for one is lawful for the nation. Then it is doubtless lawful to help one another.

The ends of public societies show it, which is mutual help. The ends of society especially require mutual help when the destruction of the community is threatened. The argument for the lawfulness of opposing force to force for the defense of public societies is more forcible than for the defense of particular persons, as the public good is more important. If it were so that all public societies must be restrained from opposing force to other nations that commit rapine and violence towards them, the whole world of mankind would be open to be laid waste. For there have been many nations that appeared forward to subdue and enslave other nations. The sixth commandment is so far from forbidding self-defense that the design of that command plainly requires it.

The very same principles on which is manifest the lawfulness and necessity of civil magistracy and of human laws, forcibly to maintain the rights of mankind in society and to use the civil sword for the punishment of those that violate those rights that are within the society, will prove the lawfulness of war. The power of the sword is, Romans 13:4, "to execute wrath upon him that doeth evil." Those that violate the rights of mankind in society are punished by the civil sword only as acting the part of enemies. If there should, instead of a single offender, arise a great number—as in a public riot or mob or rebellion—'tis lawful to punish them; and this is the same thing with here, if a particular town or city or province should offend. This is war.

If war be lawful to defend a society from domestic enemies, then doubtless if a particular man should come from a foreign country and should set himself to do mischief, he should be similarly punished. Thus the light of nature justifies war. But besides, God has abundantly shown his approbation: directing, encouraging, commanding, and ordering the affairs of war, and rewarding the defenders of the people. And that God approves of some war appears not only from the Old Testament, but the New. The New Testament approves of the civil magistracy, and of the magistrates' using the sword to restrain open violence with force. Romans 13:1–4. . . .

If it be a duty for a people to wage war for the defense of the community, then it is their duty to prosecute that war in such a manner as tends most effectually to obtain this end, not barely to stand on their defense when their enemies actually assault them. To not sufficiently defend may greatly expose 'em; they should not merely attempt to stand to defend themselves when assaulted by robbers or pirates. If it be a duty of a people to wage war, 'tis a duty to prosecute it with vigor. The sixth commandment requires it, as it tends most to save the lives of the innocent, and is in fact soonest to bring the war to an end. The good of the community, and especially the maintaining its rights, is the end of war; this end therefore must govern the management of it.

People ought not to be forward to enter into war; the occasion should be important, even be so that the public preservation requires it, as when the society is invaded. When another nation do declare war with them unjustly, or when they do that which is equivalent, or when another nation do in some very notable instances invade their rights and do persist in it, the upholding of the rights and privileges of the society requires it. . . .

Particular persons are called of God when they are called by those that are in authority, unless it be notoriously manifest that the war is unjust. In ordinary cases, particular subjects are not called to inquire. God has not made them judges. It is not practicable, and therefore, unless it be plain and notorious that the war is unjust, particular persons should act as called by God. Sometimes the professed and declared design of a war is plainly unjust, as when the declared design is persecution. But when this is not the case, and persons are particularly required by the civil authority, and when the call of the civil authority is not particular but only general—leaving it to particular persons to judge for themselves and follow their own voluntary determinations, as in gathering of an army of volunteers—then persons should look on themselves as called of God according to the best judgment they can make to be marked out in providence, as the properest persons to engage in the business that the civil authority calls them to, considering their particular circumstances and qualifications.

Proposition II. 'Tis God, and he only, that determines the event of war and gives the victory. . . .

Proposition III. When a people are called to go forth to war, 'tis their duty, by prayer and supplication, to look to God for help to maintain their cause. . . .

Proposition IV. God is ready in such a case to hear the prayers of his people, and give 'em success, when they offer up their prayers in the manner that he has appointed. . . .

It greatly concerns this land with one accord, all sorts of persons in it—magistrates, ministers and people; young and old—to go to the God of armies and pour out their prayers and supplications to him, that he would appear for us and maintain our cause in this undertaking. It is of vast importance to us that the expedition should be succeeded on many accounts. This province have put themselves to a very great expense, and before the affair is finished the expense will doubtless be yet vastly greater—doubtless several hundred thousand pounds—and it would be a great and sore judgment upon us to have all this expense frustrated.

And besides, if the enterprise should be defeated, the defeat will probably be attended with the loss of much blood and the expense of many lives: to the filling of many families and many of our towns, yea, the province in general, with mourning through the bereavement of friends and neighbors. There will probably be many made widows and many children fatherless, and many parents bereaved of dear children, and some of those that were the flower of our land cut off. Besides, the place that our forces are gone against has been a great annoyance to us. The people of this land have been more annoyed from this particular place than any other whatsoever since the commencement of the present war, and if this design is defeated there is a prospect of their being still a much greater annoyance to us. Projections have been formed and preparations been making, as we have had credible information, to annoy us from thence with a much greater force than heretofore; and if we fail in this enterprise, that will strengthen them and expose us to them many ways. We shall be greatly weakened by it: we shall be weakened as we shall be greatly impoverished and less able to be at the expense of a vigorous defense and opposition for the future, and shall be weakened in numbers and shall be greatly weakened as it will tend to dishearten us. . . .

On the other hand, if it pleases God to give us success, very great are the appearing advantages. 'Tis to be hoped that we may see most of our friends that are gone forth returning with rejoicing. We shall be delivered from a strong fortress that has been very much the nest and resort of our enemies, and shall have a very strong place in our possession that is so situated that we shall thereby be probably under vast advantages against our enemies in Canada to restrain them and distress them, and prevail against them by hindering supplies being sent to them. And our enemies that we have most reason to fear will probably be much weakened and disheartened, and will be much more afraid to molest us, lest we should be provoked to prosecute the advantage we have gained and go on with our conquests till we have subdued the neighboring country of our enemies. Our sea coasts will be much less exposed and our enemies under much less advantages to disturb us in our business on the sea, in our trade and fishery; and our eastern settlements in particular would be much less exposed. . . .

Before I conclude, I would mention two things to excite all to seek to God for success in that warlike enterprise that is the occasion of our fast.

First. How God has blasted us in such like enterprises heretofore as we have reason to think, for want of this spirit of prayer.

Second. How many remarkable instances we have in it of the success of faith and prayer in warlike undertakings. The first I shall mention is in that great pattern of believers, Abraham, called in Scripture the father of all them that believe that we have an account of in Genesis 14. The giants could not stand before them. Thus God "gave the nations before him" as is said, Isaiah 41:2. Another instance is that of the people of Israel against Amalek, Exodus 17:9–13. . . .

Such abundant encouragement is there in the Word of God. These instances show that 'tis God that disposes, and how ready he is to appear, and as it were delights to bestow great mercies of this kind and bring wonderful things in subduing mighty enemies and strong cities, and breaking the greatest power of the enemy, in answer to the believing prayers of his people that walk in his ways.

16

Treatise concerning Religious Affections (1746)

Edwards drafted his *Treatise concerning Religious Affections* in 1743, shortly after the Great Awakening of 1740–42 had faded, and revised and published it three years later. Earlier he had described the revival fervor of the Connecticut Valley in the mid-1730s and at the outset of the Great Awakening. *Religious Affections,* by contrast, was less description than analysis and assessment. He wanted especially to provide guidance in judging evidence of grace. His acuity, candor, and relevance kept the treatise in print and in the hands of generations of evangelists, theologians, seminarians, and students of the human psyche.

By the time he wrote *Religious Affections,* Edwards had soured on revivalism, which despite its initial promise seemed not to produce much lasting piety or heartfelt charity. On the contrary, there were ample signs of erratic, even bizarre religious enthusiasm all across New England, including holier-than-thou criticism from the newly enraptured that settled ministers and churches were "without grace." There were schisms in local churches and sharp condemnation, especially from prestigious Bostonians, of the whole idea of revival preaching and mass awakenings. Some of this criticism targeted Edwards as a leading instigator.

Edwards was not quite ready to jettison all efforts to transform hearts through "awakening" preaching. But the bulk of his treatise, particularly its lengthy part 12 (excerpted below), aimed mainly at the enthusiasts themselves for confusing "counterfeit zeal" with true religious affections. No one, he argued, not even ministers—certainly not the newly evangelized—can know God's work in the human heart. Claims of exceptional grace and criticism of others for lacking grace are therefore unwarranted and smack of pride. But if there is no infallible way to read human hearts, one way is better than any other: behavior that reflects the spirit and temper of Edwards's ethical model, Jesus Christ. The truly reborn will live like Christ—forgiving, bearing no grudges, trusting like children, loving one another, and, as commanded by scripture for thousands of years, helping the poor.

Edwards continued to encourage efforts to spread the gospel through, for example, writing, missionary work, and prayer, and still aspired to see hearts transformed on a large scale. He published a treatise in 1747 urging ecumenical

From *The Works of Jonathan Edwards,* vol. 2, *Religious Affections,* ed. John E. Smith (New Haven: Yale University Press, 1959), 344–57.

prayer for worldwide religious awakening, but by this time, he had become more circumspect about revivals: their fruits could be judged only over time, and only by the Christ-like lives of their participants.

Truly gracious affections differ from those affections that are false and delusive, in that they tend to, and are attended with, the lamblike, dove-like spirit and temper of Jesus Christ; or in other words, they naturally beget and promote such a spirit of love, meekness, quietness, forgiveness and mercy, as appeared in Christ.

The evidence of this in the Scripture, is very abundant. If we judge of the nature of Christianity, and the proper spirit of the gospel, by the word of God, this spirit is what may by way of eminency be called the Christian spirit; and may be looked upon as the true, and distinguishing disposition of the hearts of Christians, as Christians. When some of the disciples of Christ said something, through inconsideration and infirmity, that was not agreeable to such a spirit, Christ told them that he knew not what manner of spirit they were of, Luke 9:55, implying that this spirit that I am speaking of, is the proper spirit of his religion and kingdom. All that are truly godly, and real disciples of Christ, have this spirit in them; and not only so but they are of this spirit; it is the spirit in them; it is the spirit by which they are so possessed and governed, that it is their true and proper character. This is evident by what the wise man says (having respect plainly to such a spirit as this): "A man of understanding is of an excellent spirit" (Proverbs 17:27); and by the particular description Christ gives of the qualities and temper of such as are truly blessed that shall obtain mercy, and are God's children and heirs, "Blessed are the meek: for they shall inherit the earth. Blessed are the merciful: for they shall obtain mercy. Blessed are the peacemakers: for they shall be called the children of God" (Matthew 5:5, 7, 9).

And that this spirit is the special character of the elect of God is manifest by Colossians 3:12–13: "Put on therefore, as the elect of God, holy and beloved, bowels of mercies, kindness, humbleness of mind, meekness, long-suffering; forbearing one another, and forgiving one another." And the Apostle speaking of that temper and disposition which he speaks of as the most excellent and essential thing in Christianity, and that without which none are true Christians, and the most glorious

profession and gifts are nothing (calling this spirit by the name of charity) he describes it thus: "Charity suffereth long and is kind; charity en-
vieth not; charity vaunteth not itself, is not puffed up; doth not behave
itself unseemly; seeketh not her own; is not easily provoked; thinketh no
evil" (Corinthians 13:4–5). . . .

Everything that appertains to holiness of heart, does indeed belong
to the nature of true Christianity, and the character of Christians; but
a spirit of holiness as appearing in some particular graces, may more
especially be called the Christian spirit or temper. There are some amiable qualities and virtues that do more especially agree with the nature
of the gospel constitution, and Christian profession; because there is a
special agreeableness in them, with those divine attributes which God
has more remarkably manifested and glorified in the work of redemption by Jesus Christ, that is the grand subject of the Christian revelation;
and also a special agreeableness with those virtues that were so wonderfully exercised by Jesus Christ towards us in that affair, and the blessed
example he hath therein for us; and likewise because they are peculiarly
agreeable to the special drift and design of the work of redemption, and
the benefits we thereby receive, and the relation that it brings us into, to
God and one another. And these virtues are such as humility, meekness,
love, forgiveness, and mercy. These things therefore especially belong to
the character of Christians, as such. . . .

All true Christians behold as in a glass, the glory of the Lord, and are
changed into the same image, by his Spirit (II Corinthians. 3:18). The
elect are all predestinated to be conformed to the image of the Son of
God (Romans 8:29). . . . As we have borne the image of the first man,
that is earthly, so we must also bear the image of the heavenly. . . . Christ
is full of grace; and Christians all receive of his fullness, and grace for
grace: i.e. there is grace in Christians answering to grace in Christ, such
an answerableness as there is between the wax and the seal; there is
character for character: such kind of graces, such a spirit and temper, the
same things that belong to Christ's character, belong to theirs.

That disposition wherein Christ's character does in a special manner
consist, therein does his image in a special manner consist. Christians
that shine by reflecting the light of the Sun of Righteousness, do shine
with the same sort of brightness, the same mild, sweet and pleasant
beams. These lamps of the spiritual temple, that are enkindled by fire

from heaven, burn with the same sort of flame. The branch is of the same nature with the stock and root, has the same sap, and bears the same sort of fruit. The members have the same kind of life with the head. It would be strange if Christians should not be of the same temper and spirit that Christ is of; when they are his flesh and his bone, yea are one spirit (I Corinthians 6:17), and live so, that it is not they that live, but Christ that lives in them. . . .

True Christians are as it were clothed with the meek, quiet, and loving temper of Christ; for as many as are in Christ, have put on Christ. And in this respect the church is clothed with the Sun, not only by being clothed with his imputed righteousness, but also by being adorned with his graces (Romans 13:14). . . . The redemption of the church by Christ from the power of the devil was typified of old, by David's delivering the lamb, out of the mouth of the lion and the bear. . . .

'Tis doubtless very much on this account, that Christ represents all his disciples, all the heirs of heaven, as little children, "Suffer little children to come unto me, and forbid them not; for of such is the kingdom of heaven" (Matthew 19:14). . . . "Little children, yet a little while am I with you" (John 13:33). Little children are innocent and harmless: they don't do a great deal of mischief in the world: men need not be afraid of them: they are no dangerous sort of persons: their anger don't last long: they don't lay up injuries in high resentment entertaining deep and rooted malice. So Christians, in malice, are children (I Corinthians 4:20). Little children are not guileful and deceitful; but plain and simple: they are not versed in the arts of fiction and deceit; and are strangers to artful disguises. They are yieldable and flexible, and not willful and obstinate; don't trust to their own understanding, but rely on the instructions of parents, and others of superior understanding. Here is therefore a fit and lively emblem of the followers of the Lamb. Persons being thus like little children, is not only a thing highly commendable, and what Christians approve of, and aim at, and which some of extraordinary proficiency do attain to; but it is their universal character, and absolutely necessary in order to entering the kingdom of heaven. . . .

The directest and surest way in the world, to make a right judgment, what a holy fortitude is, in fighting with God's enemies, is to look to the captain of all God's hosts, and our great leader and example; . . . even to Jesus Christ in the time of his last sufferings; when his enemies in earth and hell made their most violent attack upon him, compassing him round on every side, like renting and roaring lions. Doubtless here we shall see the fortitude of a holy warrior and champion in the cause of God, in its highest perfection and greatest luster, and an example fit for the soldiers to follow, that fight under this captain.

But how did he show his holy boldness and valor at that time? Not in the exercise of any fiery passions; not in fierce and violent speeches, and vehemently declaiming against, and crying out of the intolerable wickedness of opposers, giving 'em their own in plain terms; but in not opening his mouth when afflicted and oppressed, in going as a lamb to the slaughter, and as a sheep before his shearers, is dumb, not opening his mouth; praying that the Father would forgive his cruel enemies, because they knew not what they did; not shedding others' blood; but with all-conquering patience and love, shedding his own. Indeed, one of his disciples, that made a forward pretense to boldness for Christ, and confidently declared he would sooner die with Christ than deny him, began to lay about him with a sword: but Christ meekly rebukes him, and heals the wound he gives.

And never was the patience, meekness, love, and forgiveness of Christ, in so glorious a manifestation, as at that time. Never did he appear so much a lamb, and never did he show so much of the dovelike spirit, as at that time. If therefore we see any of the followers of Christ, in the midst of the most violent, unreasonable and wicked opposition, of God's and his own enemies, maintaining under all this temptation, the humility, quietness, and gentleness of a lamb and the harmlessness, and love, and sweetness of a dove, we may well judge that here is a good soldier of Jesus Christ. . . .

There is a pretended boldness for Christ that arises from no better principle than pride. A man may be forward to expose himself to the dislike of the world; and even to provoke their displeasure, out of pride. For 'tis the nature of spiritual pride to cause men to seek distinction and singularity; and so oftentimes to set themselves at war with those that they call carnal, that they may be more highly exalted among their party.

True boldness for Christ is universal and overcomes all, and carries 'em above the displeasure of friends and foes; so that they will forsake all rather than Christ and will rather offend all parties, and be thought meanly of by all than offend Christ. And that duty which tries whether a man is willing to be despised by them that are of his own party and though the least worthy to be regarded by them, is a much more proper trial of his boldness for Christ, than his being forward to expose himself to the reproach of opposers. . . .

He is bold for Christ, that has Christian fortitude enough, to confess his faults openly when he has committed one that requires it, and as it were to come down upon his knees before opposers. Such things as these are a vastly greater evidence of holy boldness, than resolutely and fiercely confronting opposers.

As some are much mistaken concerning the nature of true boldness for Christ, so they are concerning Christian zeal. 'Tis indeed a flame but a sweet one: or rather it is the heat and fervor of a sweet flame. For the flame of which it is the heat, is no other than that of divine love, or Christian charity; which is the sweetest and most benevolent thing that is, or can be in the heart of man or angel. Zeal is the fervor of this flame, as it ardently and vigorously goes out towards the good that is its object, in desires of it, and pursuit after it: and so consequentially, in opposition to the evil that is contrary to it, and impedes it.

There is indeed opposition, and vigorous opposition that is a part of it, or rather is an attendant of it; but it is against *things* and not *persons*. Bitterness against the persons of men is no part of it, but is very contrary to it; inasmuch that so much the warmer true zeal is and the higher it is raised, so much the further are persons from such bitterness and so much fuller of love, both to the evil and to the good.

As appears from what has been just now observed that it is no other in its very nature and essence, than the fervor of a spirit of Christian love. And as to what opposition there is in it, to things, it is firstly and chiefly against the evil things in the person himself, who has this zeal; against the enemies of God and holiness, that are in his own heart (as these are most in his view, and what he is most to do with); and but secondarily against the sins of others. And therefore there is nothing in a true Christian zeal, that is contrary to that spirit of meekness, gentleness and love, that spirit of a little child, a lamb and dove, that has been spoken of but it is entirely agreeable to it and tends to promote it.

But to say something particularly concerning this Christian spirit I have been speaking of as exercised in these three things, forgiveness, love and mercy: I would observe that the Scripture is very clear and express concerning the absolute necessity of each of these as belonging to the temper and character of every Christian.

It is so as to a forgiving spirit, or a disposition to overlook and forgive injuries. Christ gives it to us both as a negative and positive evidence; and is express in teaching us, that if we are of such a spirit, 'tis a sign we are in a state of forgiveness and favor ourselves; and that if we are not of such a spirit, we are not forgiven of God; and seems to take special care that we should take good notice of it, and always bear it on our minds. "Forgive us our debts, as we forgive our debtors. . . . For if ye forgive men their trespasses, your heavenly Father will also forgive you: but if ye forgive not men their trespasses, neither will your Father forgive your trespasses" (Matthew 6:12, 14–15). . . .

And that all true saints are of a loving benevolent and beneficent temper, the Scripture is very plain and abundant. Without it the apostle tells us, though we should speak with the tongues of men and angels, we are as a sounding brass or a tinkling cymbal: and that though we have the gift of prophecy, and understand all mysteries, and all knowledge; yet without this spirit we are nothing. And there is no one virtue or disposition of the mind, that is so often, and so expressly insisted on, in the marks that are laid down in the New Testament, whereby to know true Christians. 'Tis often given as a sign that is peculiarly distinguishing, by which all may know Christ's disciples, and by which they may know themselves and is often laid down, both as a negative and positive evidence. Christ calls the law of love, by way of eminency, his commandment (John 13:34). . . .

The Beloved Disciple [John] who had so much of this sweet temper himself, abundantly insists on it in his Epistles. There is none of the apostles, is so much in laying down express signs of grace, for professors to try themselves by, as he; and in his signs, he insists scarcely on anything else, but a spirit of Christian love, and an agreeable practice; "He that saith he is in the light, and hateth his brother, is in darkness even until now. He that loveth his brother abideth in the light, and there is none occasion of stumbling in him" (John 2:9–10). . . .

And the Scripture is as plain as it is possible it should be, that none are true saints, but those whose true character it is, that they are of a disposition to pity and relieve their fellow creatures, that are poor, indigent, and afflicted. "The righteous showeth mercy, and giveth" (Psalms 37:21): "He is ever merciful and lendeth" (verse 26). "A good man showeth favor, and lendeth (Psalms 112:5). "He hath dispersed abroad, and given to the poor" (verse 9). "He that honoreth God, hath mercy on the poor" (Proverbs 14:31). "The righteous giveth, and spareth not" (Proverbs 21:26). "He judged the cause of the poor and needy: then it was well with him: was not this to know me, saith the Lord?" (Jeremiah 22:16). "Pure religion and undefiled before God and the Father, is this: to visit the fatherless and widows in their affliction," etc. (James 1:27). "For I desired mercy, and not sacrifice; and the knowledge of God, more than burnt-offerings" (Hosea 6:6).

"Blessed are the merciful, for they shall obtain mercy" (Matthew 5:7). "I seek not by commandment, but by occasion of the forwardness of others, and to prove the sincerity of your love" (II Corinthians 8:8). . . . "What does it profit my brethren, though a man saith he hath faith, and have not works? Can faith save him? If a brother or sister be naked, and destitute of daily food, and one of you say unto them, depart in peace, be you warmed and filled; notwithstanding ye give them not those things which are needful for the body; what doth it profit?" (James 2:13–16). "Whoso hath this world's goods, and seeth his brother have need, and shutteth up his bowels of compassion from him, how dwelleth the love of God in him?" (I John 3:17).

Christ in that description he gives us of the Day of Judgment, Matthew 25 (which is the most particular that we have in all the Bible): represents that judgment will be passed at that day, according as men have been found to have been of a merciful spirit and practice, or otherwise. Christ's design in giving such a description of the process of that day, is plainly to possess all his followers with that apprehension, that unless this was their spirit and practice, there was no hope of their being accepted and owned by him, at that day. Therefore this is an apprehension that we ought to be possessed with. . . .

Thus we see how full, clear and abundant, the evidence from Scripture is, that those who are truly gracious, are under the government of that lamblike, dovelike spirit of Jesus Christ. And that this is essentially and eminently the nature of the saving grace of the gospel, and the proper spirit of true Christianity.

17

Sermon: "A Strong Rod Broken and Withered" (1748)

Edwards preached "A Strong Rod" as a memorial sermon on the death of his uncle Colonel John Stoddard. One of Northampton's leading landowners, a frequently elected representative to town offices and the colonial assembly in Boston, an effective diplomat and militia leader, Stoddard was a strong supporter of Edwards throughout his Northampton ministry. Edwards seldom preached on personal matters, and on balance did not do so here. But the conclusion of the sermon, with its references to private conversations on religion and ethics, suggests that he would sorely miss the colonel's wisdom, strength, and experience.

Edwards's main concern, as in his political sermons of the early 1730s, was to delineate the traits of a good leader. Most would have been familiar to the congregation given his oft-expressed values, though they were on the whole secular rather than spiritual. High on the list was sterling personal capacity and character—a talent for public affairs, for example, including managerial skills, ability to compromise, and knowledge of human nature. Equally important were devotion to public rather than private interest, and honor and integrity in promoting public happiness and prosperity. On the negative side, this meant resisting the bribes and pressures of the "great," not harming "the poor," and refusing to seek personal gain. A good leader would make policy openly rather than secretly, and, though principled, would be willing to compromise. Ideally, Edwards argued, a leader needed to enjoy high stature by virtue of wealth, education, and lineage, which would lend weight to his decisions and incline people to accept them. Experience was helpful as a means of understanding constitutional issues and patterns of diplomacy. Piety, one of the goals of public policy, mattered as well.

These, Edwards concluded, were precisely the traits of John Stoddard. Historians have largely endorsed this judgment: Stoddard was an able and conscientious leader of an Edwardsean stripe. That stripe involved a lot of deference, still common in British North America, but Edwards justified his position on leadership not on the basis of biblical injunction or aristocratic entitlement but by logic and common sense. And while Edwards clearly valued deference, he also knew that Stoddard, like everyone else, had sometimes been voted down when he stood for office, a process and an outcome implying a significant measure of public participation that Edwards never criticized, however much he might disagree with the results.

From *The Works of Jonathan Edwards*, vol. 25, *Sermons and Discourses, 1743–1758,* ed. Wilson H. Kimnach (New Haven: Yale University Press, 2006), 312–29.

Her strong rods were broken and withered. (Ezekiel 19:12)

It is very remarkable that such a strong rod should grow out of a weak vine: but so it had been in Israel, through God's extraordinary blessing, in times past. Though the nation is spoken of here, and frequently elsewhere, as weak and helpless in itself, and entirely dependent as a vine, that is the weakest of all trees that can't support itself by its own strength, and never stands but as it leans on or hangs by something else that is stronger than itself; yet God had caused many of her sons to be strong rods fit for scepters; he had raised up in Israel many able and excellent princes and magistrates in days past, that had done worthily in their day. . . .

One qualification of rulers whence they may properly be denominated "strong rods," is great ability for the management of public affairs. When they that stand in place of public authority are men of great natural abilities, when they are men of uncommon strength of reason and largeness of understanding; especially when they have remarkably a genius for government, a peculiar turn of mind fitting them to gain an extraordinary understanding in things of that nature, giving ability, in an especial manner, for insight into the mysteries of government, and discerning those things wherein the public welfare or calamity consists, and the proper means to avoid the one and promote the other;

an extraordinary talent at distinguishing what is right and just, from that which is wrong and unequal, and to see through the false colors with which justice is often disguised, and unravel the false and subtle arguments and cunning sophistry that is often made use of to defend iniquity; and when they have not only great natural abilities in these respects, but when their abilities and talents have been improved by study, learning, observation and experience; and when by these means they have obtained great actual knowledge;

when they have acquired great skill in public affairs, and things requisite to be known, in order to their wise, prudent and effectual management; when they have obtained a great understanding of men and things, a great knowledge of human nature, and of the way of accommodating themselves to it, so as most effectually to influence it to wise purposes;

when they have obtained a very extensive knowledge of men with whom they are concerned in the management of public affairs, either those that have joint concern in government, or those that are to be governed; and when they have also obtained a very full and particular understanding of the state and circumstances of the county or people that they have the care of, and know well their laws and constitution; and what their circumstances require; and likewise have a great knowledge of the people of neighbor nations, states, or provinces, with whom they have occasion to be concerned in the management of public affairs committed to them; these things all contribute to the rendering those that are in authority fit to be denominated "strong rods." . . .

When they have not only great understanding, but *largeness of heart, and a greatness and nobleness of disposition,* this is another qualification that belongs to the character of a strong rod.

Those that are by divine providence set in place of public authority and rule are called "gods," and "sons of the Most High" (Psalms 82:6). And therefore 'tis peculiarly unbecoming them to be of a mean spirit, a disposition that will admit of their doing those things that are sordid and vile; as when they are persons of a narrow, private spirit, that may be found in little tricks and intrigues to promote their private interest, will shamefully defile their hands, to gain a few pounds, are not ashamed to nip and bite others, grind the faces of the poor, and screw upon their neighbors; and will take advantage of their authority or commission to line their own pockets with what is fraudulently taken or withheld from others. When a man in authority is of such a mean spirit, it weakens his authority, and makes him justly contemptible in the eyes of men, and is utterly inconsistent with his being a strong rod.

But on the contrary, it greatly establishes his authority, and causes others to stand in awe of him, when they see him to be a man of *greatness of mind,* one that abhors those things that are mean and sordid, and not capable of a compliance with them; one that is of a *public spirit,* and not of a private narrow disposition, a man of honor, and not a man of mean artifice and clandestine management, for filthy lucre, and one that abhors trifling and impertinence, or to waste away his time, that should be spent in the service of God, his king, or his country, in vain amusements and diversions, and in the pursuit of the gratifications of sensual appetites. . . .

When those that are in authority are endowed with much of a spirit of government, this is another thing that entitles them to the denomination of "strong rods." When they not only are men of great understanding and wisdom in affairs that appertain to government but have also a peculiar talent at using their knowledge, and exerting themselves in this great and important business, according to their great understanding in it; when they are men of eminent fortitude, and are not afraid of the faces of men, are not afraid to do the part that properly belongs to them as rulers, though they meet with great opposition, and the spirits of men are greatly irritated by it; when they have a spirit of *resolution and activity,* so as to keep the wheels of government in proper motion, and to cause judgment and justice to run down as a mighty stream; when they have not only a great knowledge of government, and the things that belong to it in the theory but it is as it were natural to them to apply the various powers and faculties with which God has endowed them, and the knowledge they have obtained by study and observation, to that business, so as to perform it most advantageously and effectually. . . .

And lastly, it also contributes to that strength of a man in authority, by which he may be denominated a "strong rod," when he is *in such circumstances,* as give him advantage for the exercise of his strength for the public good; as his being a person of honorable descent, of a distinguished education, his being a man of estate, one that is advanced in years, one that has long been in authority, so that it is become as it were natural for the people to pay him deference, to reverence him, to be influenced and governed by him, and submit to his authority; his being extensively known, and much honored and regarded abroad; his being one of a good presence, majesty of countenance, decency of behavior, becoming one in authority; of forcible speech, etc. These things add to his strength and increase his ability and advantage to serve his generation. . . .

Almost all the prosperity of a public society, and civil community does, under God, depend on their rulers. They are like the main springs or wheels in a machine; that keep every part in their due motion, and are in the body *politic,* as the vitals in the body *natural,* and as the pillars and foundation in a building. Civil rulers are called the "foundations of the earth" (Psalms 82:5 and 11:13).

The prosperity of a people depends more on their rulers than is commonly imagined. As they have the public society under their care and power, so they have advantage to promote the public interest every way; and if they are such rulers as have been spoken of, they are some of the greatest blessings to the public. Their influence has a tendency to promote their wealth, and cause their temporal possessions and blessings to abound. And to promote virtue amongst them, and so to unite them one to another in peace and mutual benevolence, and make them happy in society, each one the instrument of his neighbor's quietness, comfort and prosperity; and by these means to advance their reputation and honor in the world; and which is much more, to promote their spiritual and eternal happiness. Therefore the Wise Man says, Ecclesiastes 10:17, "Blessed are thou, O land, when thy king is the son of nobles."

We have a remarkable instance and evidence of the happy and great influence of such a strong rod as has been described, to promote the universal prosperity of a people, in the history of the reign of Solomon, though many of the people were uneasy under his government, and thought him too rigorous in his administrations: see I Kings 12:4. . . .

Government is necessary to defend communities from miseries from within themselves; from the prevalence of intestine discord, mutual injustice and violence. The members of the society continually making a prey one of another, without any defense one from another. Rulers are the heads of union in public societies, that hold the parts together; without which nothing else is to be expected than that the members of the society will be continually divided against themselves, every one acting the part of an enemy to his neighbor, every one's hand against every man, and every man's hand against him; going on in remediless and endless broils and jarring, till the society be utterly dissolved and broken in pieces, and life itself, in the neighborhood of our fellow creatures, becomes miserable and intolerable. . . .

As government is absolutely necessary, so there is a necessity of strong rods in order to it: the business being such as requires persons so qualified; no other being sufficient for, or well capable of the government of public societies: and therefore those public societies are miserable that have not such strong rods for scepters to rule; Ecclesiastes 10:16, "Woe to thee, O land, when thy king is a child." . . .

I come now to apply these things to our own case, under the late awful frown of divine providence upon us, in removing by death that honorable person in public rule and authority, an inhabitant of this town, and belonging to this congregation and church, who died at Boston the last Lord's day. . . .

He was probably one of the ablest politicians that ever New England bred: he had a very uncommon insight into human nature, and a marvelous ability to penetrate into the particular tempers and dispositions of such as he had to deal with, and to discern the fittest way of treating them, so as most effectually to influence them to any good and wise purpose.

And never, perhaps, was there a person that had a more extensive and thorough knowledge of the state of this land, and its public affairs, and of persons, and their circumstances, and what their circumstances required: he discerned the diseases of this body, and what were the proper remedies, as an able and masterly physician. He had a great acquaintance with the neighboring colonies, and also the neighbor nations on this continent with whom we are concerned in our public affairs: he had a far greater knowledge than any other person in the land of the several nations of Indians in these northern parts of America. . . .

And besides his knowledge of things belonging to his particular calling as a ruler, he had also a great degree of understanding in things belonging to his general calling as a Christian. He was no inconsiderable divine: he was a wise casuist [applying ethical principles according to the case], as I know by the great help I have found from time to time, by his judgment and advice in cases of conscience, wherein I have consulted him: and indeed I scarce knew the divine that I ever found more able to help and enlighten the mind in such cases than he. And he had no small degree of knowledge in things pertaining to experimental [heartfelt] religion; but was wont to discourse on such subjects, not only with accurate doctrinal distinctions, but as one intimately and feelingly acquainted with these things. . . .

The greatness and honorableness of his disposition, was answerable to the largeness of his understanding: he was naturally of a great mind: in this respect he was truly the "son of nobles" (Ecclesiastes 10:16). He greatly abhorred things which were mean and sordid, and seemed to be incapable of a compliance with them. How far was he from trifling and impertinence in his conversation? How far from a busy, meddling disposition? How far from any sly and clandestine management to fill his pockets with what was fraudulently withheld, or violently squeezed from the laborer, soldier or inferior officer? How far from taking advantage from his commission or authority, or any superior power he had in his hands? Or the ignorance, dependence or necessities of others to add to his own gains with what property belonged to them, and with what they might justly expect as a proper reward for any of their services? How far was he from secretly taking bribes offered to induce him to favor any man in his cause, or by his power or interest to promote his being advanced to any place of public trust, honor or profit? How greatly did he abhor lying and prevaricating? And how immovably steadfast was he to exact truth? His hatred of those things that were mean and sordid was so apparent and well known, that it was evident that men dreaded to appear in anything of that nature in his presence.

He was a man remarkably of a public spirit, a true lover of his country, and greatly abhorred the sacrificing the public welfare to private interest. . . .

But though he was one that was great among men, exalted above others in abilities and greatness of mind, and in place of rule, and feared not the faces of men, yet *he feared God*. He was strictly conscientious in his conduct, both in public and private. I never knew the man that seemed more steadfastly and immovably to act by principle, and according to rules and maxims, established and settled in his mind by the dictates of his judgment and conscience. He was a man of strict justice and fidelity; faithfulness was eminently his character: some of his greatest opponents, that have been of the contrary party to him in public affairs, yet have openly acknowledged this of him, that he was a faithful man.

He was remarkably faithful in his public trusts: he would not basely betray his trust from fear or favor: it was in vain to expect it, however men might oppose him or neglect him, and how great soever they were. Nor would he neglect the public interest, wherein committed to him, for the sake of his own ease, but diligently and laboriously watched and labored for it night and day. And he was faithful in private affairs as well as public: he was a most faithful friend; faithful to anyone that in any case asked his counsel: and his fidelity might be depended on in whatever affairs he undertook for any of his neighbors. . . .

Added to all these things, that have been mentioned to render him eminently a "strong rod," he was attended with many circumstances which tended to give him advantage for the exerting of his strength for the public good. He was honorably descended, was a man of considerable substance, had been long in authority, was extensively known and honored abroad, was high in the esteem of the many tribes of Indians in the neighborhood of the British colonies, and so had great influence upon them above any other man in New England. God had endowed him with a comely presence, and majesty of countenance, becoming the great qualities of his mind, and the place in which God had set him.

18

Sermon: "Farewell Sermon" (1750)

The Northampton congregation voted in the spring of 1750 to "separate from" Edwards, its longtime minister. There had long been signs of a rift: disagreements over planning for a new meeting house, over Edwards's insistence that everyone sign the 1742 covenant, over his criticism of young men in the town for teasing girls with a midwifery book, over the town's repeated refusal to fix the minister's salary, which had depreciated mightily from inflation and now had to stretch over eleven children and a stream of visitors and ministerial apprentices. Edwards also announced in 1746 that he was changing the rules for admission to communion: from then on, people were to publicly attest rebirth and exhibit commensurate behavior before taking part in the sacrament, a position that apparently rankled enough church members to trigger dismissal.

Edwards was reflective and subdued in this sermon, observing that things are in constant flux, and that towns, churches, and nations as well as people change and become disunited. But he did not dwell much on what had happened. He cast events instead in a larger framework, observing that this was not in truth the last farewell. There was another yet to come, on Judgment Day at Christ's final evaluation of motives and behavior. Then there would be special scrutiny of souls who had been close in life—for example, ministers and people. We should therefore, he argued, turn this moment from guilty strife to blessed peace. Once at judgment it will be too late.

Edwards did not change his mind about communion. He did not wholly exempt himself from judgment as to whether he had been a good father to his children, the congregation, as ministers should be. He clearly thought the congregation more culpable but added that only God could judge. And he urged his supporters in the late controversy to bury their grudges and remain meek. A contentious people, he preached in 1750 as in 1726, is a miserable people. Love all men of whatever party or opinion. Love one another.

Dismissal brought financial hardship. When Edwards moved to the frontier village of Stockbridge the following year to teach and preach to Indian and colonial residents, his daughters helped to make ends meet by selling small craft items. Edwards brooded at times about a different outcome, once writing that if women, young people, and the uneducated had been able to vote, he might have won out in Northampton, suggesting that there should be, at times, a wider franchise—more democracy rather than less. There may have been, too, an indirect expression of hope that he had touched the excluded.

From *The Works of Jonathan Edwards*, vol. 25, *Sermons and Discourses, 1743–1758,* ed. Wilson H. Kimnach (New Haven: Yale University Press, 2006), 457–93.

DOCTRINE: *Ministers and the people that have been under their care, must meet one another, before Christ's tribunal, at the day of judgment.*

Ministers and the people that have been under their care, must be parted in this world, how well soever they have been united: if they are not separated before, they must be parted by death: and they may be separated while life is continued. We live in a world of change, where nothing is certain or stable: and where a little time, a few revolutions of the sun, brings to pass strange things, surprising alterations, in particular persons, in families, in towns and churches, in countries and nations.

It often happens, that those who seem most united, in a little time are most disunited, and at the greatest distance. Thus ministers and people, between whom there has been the greatest mutual regard and strictest union, may not only differ in their judgments, and be alienated in affection: but one may rend from the other, and all relation between them be dissolved; the minister may be removed to a distant place, and they may never have any more to do one with another in this world. But if it be so, there is one meeting more that they must have, and that is in the last great day of accounts. . . .

Although the whole world will be then present, all mankind of all generations gathered in one vast assembly, with all of the angelic nature, both elect and fallen angels; yet we need not suppose, that everyone will have a distinct and particular knowledge of each individual of the whole assembled multitude, which will undoubtedly consist of many millions of millions. Though 'tis probable that men's capacities will be much greater than in their present state, yet they will not be infinite: though their understanding and comprehension will be vastly extended, yet men will not be deified. There will probably be a very enlarged view, that particular persons will have of the various parts and members of that vast assembly, and so of the proceedings of that great day: but yet it must need be, that according to the nature of finite minds, some persons and some things, at that day shall fall more under the notice of particular persons, than others; and this . . . according as they shall have a nearer concern with some than others, in the transactions of that day.

There will be special reason, why those who have had special concerns together in this world in their state of probation, and whose mutual affairs will be then to be tried and judged should especially be set in one another's view. Thus we may suppose, that rulers and subjects, earthly judges and those whom they have judged, neighbors who have had mutual converse, dealings and contests, heads of families and their children and servants, shall then meet, and in a peculiar distinction be set together: And especially will it be thus with ministers and their people. . . . These shall be in each others' view, shall distinctly know each other, and shall have particular notice one of another at that time. . . .

Now sinners in the congregation meet their ministers in a state wherein they are capable of a saving change, capable of being turned, through God's blessing on the ministrations and labors of their pastor, from the power of Satan unto God, and being brought out of a state of guilt, condemnation and wrath, to a state of peace and favor with God, to the enjoyment of the privileges of his children, and a title to their eternal inheritance.

And saints now meet their ministers with great remains of corruption, and sometimes under great spiritual difficulties and affliction: and therefore are yet the proper subjects of means of an happy alternation of their state, consisting in a great freedom from these things; which they have reason to hope for in the way of an attendance on ordinances; and of which God is pleased commonly to make his ministers the instruments. And ministers and their people now meet in order to the bringing to pass such happy changes; they are the great benefits sought in their solemn meetings in this world.

But when they shall meet together at the day of judgment, it will be far otherwise. They will not then meet in order to the use of means for the bringing to effect any such changes; for they will all meet in an unchangeable state. Sinners will be in an unchangeable state: they who then shall be under the guilt and power of sin and have the wrath of God abiding on them, shall be beyond all remedy or possibility of change, and shall meet their ministers without any hopes of relief or remedy, or getting any good by their means. And as for the saints, they will be already perfectly delivered from all their before-remaining corruption, temptation and calamities of every kind, and set forever out of their reach; and no deliverance, no happy alteration will remain to be accomplished in the way of the use of means of grace, under the administration of ministers. . . .

The meeting, at the last day, of ministers and the people that have been under their care, will not be attended by anyone with a careless heedless heart.

With such an heart are their meetings often attended in this world, by many persons, having little regard to him whom they pretend unitedly to adore in their solemn duties of his public worship, taking little heed to their own thoughts or the frame of their minds, not attending to the business they are engaged in, or considering the end for which they are come together: but the meeting at that great day will be very different; there will not be one careless heart, no sleeping, no wandering of mind from the great concern of the meeting, no inattentiveness to the business of the day, no regardlessness of the presence they are in, or of those great things which they shall hear from Christ at that meeting, or that they formerly heard from him and of him by their ministers. . . .

The greater part of you who are professors of godliness have (to use the phrase of the Apostle [Paul, in II Corinthians 1:14]) "acknowledged me in part": you have heretofore acknowledged me to be your spiritual father, the instrument of the greatest good to you that ever is, or can be obtained by any of the children of men. Consider of that day, when you and I shall meet before our Judge, when it shall be examined whether you have had from me the treatment which is due of spiritual children, and whether you have treated me as you ought to have treated a spiritual father. As the relation of a natural parent brings great obligations on children in the sight of God; so much more, in many respects, does the relation of a spiritual father bring great obligations on such, whose conversion and eternal salvation they suppose God has made them the instruments of. . . .

Whoever may hereafter stand related to you as your spiritual guide, my desire and prayer is, that the great Shepherd of the sheep would have a special respect to you, and be your guide (for there is none teacheth like him), and that he who is the infinite fountain of light, would "open your eyes, and turn you from darkness unto light, and from the power of Satan unto God, that you may receive forgiveness of sins, and inheritance among them that are sanctified through faith that is in Christ" (Acts 26:18); that so, in that great day, when I shall meet you again before your Judge and mine, we may meet in joyful and glorious circumstances, never to be separated anymore. . . .

As you would seek the future prosperity of this society, 'tis of vast importance that you should avoid contention.

A contentious people will be a miserable people. The contentions which have been among you, since I first became your pastor, have been one of the greatest burdens I have labored under in the course of my ministry: not only the contentions you have had with me, but those which you have had one with another, about your lands, and other concerns. Because I knew that contention, heat of spirit, evil speaking, and things of the like nature, were directly contrary to the spirit of Christianity, and did in a peculiar manner tend to drive away God's Spirit from a people, and to render all means of grace ineffectual, as well as to destroy a people's outward comfort and welfare.

Let me therefore earnestly exhort you, as you would seek your own future good, hereafter to watch against a contentious spirit. "If you would see good days, seek peace and ensue [closely follow] it" (I Peter 3:10–11). Let the contention which has lately been about the terms of Christian communion, as it has been the greatest of your contention, so be the last of them. I would, now I am preaching my farewell sermon, say to you as the Apostle to the Corinthians, (II Corinthians 13:11), "Finally, brethren, farewell. Be perfect: be of one mind: live in peace; and the God of love and peace shall be with you."

And here I would particularly advise those, that have adhered to me in the late controversy, to watch over their spirits, and avoid all bitterness towards others. Your temptations are in some respects the greatest; because what has been lately done is grievous to you. But however wrong you may think others have done, maintain, with great diligence and watchfulness, a Christian meekness and sedateness of spirit: and labor, in this respect, to excel others who are of the contrary part: and this will be the best victory. . . .

Therefore let nothing be done through strife or vainglory: indulge no revengeful spirit in any wise; but watch and pray against it: and by all means in your power, seek the prosperity of this town: and never think you behave yourselves as becomes Christians, but when you sincerely and fervently love all men of whatever party or opinion, and whether friendly or unkind, just or injurious, to you, or your friends, or to the cause and kingdom of Christ.

19

Letter to Speaker Thomas Hubbard (1751)

Edwards spent most of the last seven years of his life in Stockbridge, Massachusetts, as a missionary to Native Americans. The Stockbridge Indians came to love him and his wife, and Edwards remarked more than once that even though most had not converted, they showed more Christian character than many of his white parishioners back in Northampton.

During these years in Stockbridge, Edwards expended considerable time and effort defending Indians against greedy whites who were manipulating the Stockbridge mission for their own benefit. Despite recurring health problems and public vilification of his efforts, Edwards wrote numerous letters to Boston and London pleading for his Indian parishioners' rights to education and justice. He obtained land and had it plowed for Indian families, for example, so that they could send their children to school, and made sure that five Indian boys found lodgings in white homes so they could receive an education. Edwards took at least one of the boys into his own home.

Once a week, the missionary theologian sat the Stockbridge Indian children down for instruction in religion, experimenting with new methods that emphasized narrative and Socratic questioning instead of rote learning, which had been the customary method.

This is an excerpt from a long letter to the speaker of the Massachusetts House of Representatives. In it we see Edwards's esteem for the character of a Mohawk chief, and his concern for the schooling, housing, food, and clothing for Indians and their children. He sought the best methods for teaching their children English, so that they could cope with their English-speaking neighbors. We also see here his desire for the training of Indian pastors for Indian congregations.

Stockbridge, August 31, 1751
Honored Sir,

. . . In general the aspect of divine providence appears exceeding favorable on the design [of educating Indians at a school in Stockbridge]; some of the chiefs of the Mohawks seemed to be much engaged in the

From *The Works of Jonathan Edwards,* vol. 16, *Letters and Personal Writings,* ed. George S. Claghorn (New Haven: Yale University Press, 1998), 395–405.

design; especially Abraham Conaughstansey, Hendrick's elder brother [Hendrick was a Mohawk chief], who I can't but look upon as a remarkable man; and in many things he has done seems to manifest great solidity, prudence, and acts very much as a person endowed with [the] humility, simplicity, self-denial and zeal of a true Christian. . . .

There are many things, which, in the present situation of this affair [of the school], greatly need to be done without delay. The boarding school needs much to be done to it. The house, furniture, and school itself should be in better order. The Indians themselves took notice of the deficiencies and irregularities. The house is in [a] miserable state; and much needs to be done to it to finish it. And not only so, but there is a necessity of the house being enlarged. . . . And the house should be furnished with seats, writing tables, and beds and bed clothes, for the children. Mean lodging will do; yet they should be such as that they may be kept clean and warm. . . .

I would also humbly propose that a young gentleman, a scholar, a man of good genius and of fervent piety, be sought for and sent hither as soon as possible, to be learning the Mohawk language, to fit him to be a missionary (if need be, to go amongst the Six Nations in their own country); in the meantime, to be assisting in instructing the Indians and their children here, in all necessary knowledge, and teaching two or three of the forwardest and most promising of the Indian boys, in order to their being brought up to learning and fitted for the ministry. . . .

One of the greatest and most hurtful defects in the method of instruction in the schools here is that no more effectual measures are taken to teach the [Indian] children to the English tongue. The instructions that have been given at school here this fifteen years past, have been in a great measure in vain for want of this. The children learn to read, to make such sounds on the sight of such marks; but know nothing what they say, and having neither profit nor entertainment by what they read, they neglect it when they leave school, and quickly lose [it].

There are but two ways to remedy this mischief: either the bringing in a number of English children into the school with the Indians; or the putting the Indian children, while young, into good English families, where they should hear nothing but English, and after they have been there a year or two, then return 'em into the school here. . . .

It happens from time to time, that the Mohawks and their instructors are run out of provisions, and have nothing to eat. Now this week they have had nothing to eat but squash and Indian corn and bread. Something must also be done at providing clothing for others of the members of the school. And when the Indians have their lands laid out, there will a necessity of a great deal of care to be taken of 'em at their first settlement, by helping them, at first, in bringing to their land, etc.

20
Moral Philosophy: *The Nature of True Virtue* (1756–57)

Edwards wrote *The Nature of True Virtue* and two other treatises while work-ing in Stockbridge, where he had fewer pastoral duties and less travel to other preaching engagements than in Northampton, and thus more time to write. *True Virtue,* completed in 1757, less than two years before his death, was his principal contribution to the philosophical debates about human nature and morality that were then swirling through Enlightenment Europe. The treatise did not rely on biblical injunction and quotation the way many of his pre-Stockbridge writings had. Nor did it mention the afterlife. While it discussed the "Divine Being" and love of God, its primary focus was on ethical behavior or love—"virtue"—in this world.

Edwards argued that love of God, which includes hearty acknowledgment of God's excellence and greatness and beauty, is essential to moral behavior that is genuinely all-encompassing—that is, "true." Most theorists at the time thought that God had implanted in humans an instinctive sense of natural moral law so that everyone would know right from wrong, and that this would incline them to honesty, loyalty, respect for life, pity for the suffering, and so forth. Edwards agreed with this but thought it would only result in a secondary, self-centered, or "private," virtue rather than an all-encompassing, primary "public" virtue. If people love God ("Being"), who is eminently, irresistibly loveable because infi-nitely beautiful, they will love by extension all of God's creation and creatures ("being"). They will in this way, and only in this way, achieve "true virtue," as opposed to a virtue based on the self or on extensions of the self such as family, town, party, or even nation. These may be desirable because they at least include more than just oneself. But in the end, they exclude and are not therefore "true."

True Virtue was an attempt, employing the language of eighteenth-century logic and a distinctive concept of beauty, to return a God of beauty and power to the center of philosophers' consideration of ethics and morality. It was also a summation of nearly everything Edwards had preached over the course of his career. Love God without reserve. Let a vision of God's beauty enable you to transcend self-centeredness and worldliness. Love one another.

From *The Works of Jonathan Edwards,* vol. 8, *Ethical Writings,* ed. Paul Ramsey (New Ha-ven: Yale University Press, 1989), 540–41, 550–51, 554, 557–58, 618.

There is a general and a particular beauty. By a "particular" beauty I mean that by which a thing appears beautiful when considered only with regard to its connection with, and tendency to some particular things within a limited and, as it were, a private sphere. And a "general" beauty is that by which a thing appears beautiful when viewed most perfectly, comprehensively and universally, with regard to all its tendencies, and its connections with everything it stands related to. The former may be without and against the latter. . . .

That only, therefore, is what I mean by true virtue, which is that, belonging to the heart of an intelligent being, that is beautiful by a general beauty, or beautiful in a comprehensive view as it is in itself, and as related to everything that it stands in connection with. And therefore when we are inquiring concerning the nature of true virtue, viz. wherein this true and general beauty of the heart does most essentially consist, this is my answer to the inquiry—

True virtue most essentially consists in benevolence to Being in general. Or perhaps to speak more accurately, it is that consent, propensity and union of heart to Being in general, that is immediately exercised in a general good will. . . .

What can it consist in, but a consent and good will to Being in general? Beauty does not consist in discord and dissent, but in consent and agreement. And if every intelligent being is some way related to Being in general, and is a part of the universal system of existence; and so stands in connection with the whole, what can its general and true beauty be, but its union and consent with the great whole?

If any such thing can be supposed as an union of heart to some particular being, or number of beings, disposing it to benevolence to a private circle or system of beings, which are but a small part of the whole; not implying a tendency to an union with the great system, and not all inconsistent with enmity towards Being in general; this I suppose not to be of the nature of true virtue; although it may in some respects be good, and may appear beautiful in a confined and contracted view of things. . . . But my meaning is that no affections towards particular persons, or beings, are of the nature of true virtue but such as arise from a generally benevolent temper, or from that habit or frame of mind, wherein consists a disposition to love Being in general. . . .

From what has been said, 'tis evident that true virtue must chiefly consist in love to God; the Being of beings, infinitely the greatest and best of beings. This appears, whether we consider the primary or secondary ground of virtuous love. . . . The first objective ground of that love, wherein true virtue consists, is Being, simply considered; and as a necessary consequence of this, that being who has the most of being, or the greatest share of universal existence, has proportionably the greatest share of virtuous benevolence, so far as such a being is exhibited to the faculties of our minds, other things being equal. But God has infinitely the greatest share of existence, or is infinitely the greatest being. So that all other being, even that of all created things whatsoever, throughout the whole universe, is as nothing in comparison of the Divine Being.

And if we consider the secondary ground of love, viz. beauty or moral excellency, the same thing will appear. For as God is infinitely the greatest being, so he is allowed to be infinitely the most beautiful and excellent: and all the beauty to be found throughout the whole creation, is but the reflection of the diffused beams of that Being who hath an infinite fullness of brightness and glory. God's beauty is infinitely more valuable than that of all other beings upon both those accounts mentioned, viz. the *degree* of his virtue and the greatness of the being possessed of this virtue.

And God has sufficiently exhibited himself, in his being, his infinite greatness and excellency: and has given us faculties, whereby we are capable of plainly discovering immense superiority to all other beings in these respects. Therefore he that has true virtue, consisting in benevolence to Being in general, and in that complacence in virtue, or moral beauty, and benevolence to virtuous being, must necessarily have a supreme love to God, both of benevolence and complacence. And all true virtue must radically and essentially, and as it were summarily, consist in this. Because God is not only infinitely greater and more excellent than all other being, but he is the head of the universal system of existence; the foundation and fountain of all being and all beauty; from whom all is perfectly derived, and on whom all is most absolutely and perfectly dependent; *of whom,* and *through whom,* and *to whom* is all being and all perfection; and whose being and beauty is as it were the sum and comprehension of all existence and excellence: much more than the sun is the fountain and summary comprehension of all the light and brightness of the day. . . .

And therefore let it be supposed that some beings, by natural instinct or by some other means, have a determination of mind to union and benevolence to a *particular person* or *private system,* which is but a small part of the universal system of being: and that this disposition or determination of mind is independent on, or not subordinate to, benevolence to *Being in general.* Such a determination, disposition, or affection of mind is not of the nature of true virtue.

This is allowed by all with regard to *self-love,* in which good will is confined to one single person only. And there are the same reasons why any other private affection of good will, though extending to a society of persons independent of, and unsubordinate to, benevolence to the universality, should not be esteemed truly virtuous. For, notwithstanding it extends to a number of persons which taken together are more than a single person, yet the whole falls infinitely short of the universality of existence; and if but in the scales with it, has no greater proportion to it than a single person. . . .

With respect to the manner in which a virtuous love in created beings, one to another, is dependent on, and derived from love to God, this will appear by a proper consideration of what has been said; that it is sufficient to render love to any created being virtuous if it arise from the temper of mind wherein consists a disposition to love God supremely. Because it appears from what has been already observed, all that love to particular beings which is the fruit of a benevolent propensity of heart to Being in general, is virtuous love. . . . A benevolent propensity of heart to Being in general, and a temper or disposition to love God supremely, are in effect the same thing. Therefore, if love to a created being comes from that temper or propensity of the heart, it is virtuous. . . .

Genuine virtue prevents that increase of the habits of pride and sensuality, which tend to overbear and greatly diminish the exercises of the . . . useful and necessary principles of nature. And a principle of general benevolence softens and sweetens the mind and makes it more susceptible of the proper influence and exercise of the gentler natural instincts, and directs every one into its proper channel, and determines the exercise to the proper manner and measure, and guides all to the best purposes.

FOR FURTHER READING

More on Edwards's Social Vision

Hall, Richard A. S. *The Neglected Northampton Texts of Jonathan Edwards: Edwards on Society and Politics.* Lewiston, N.Y.: Edwin Mellen, 1990.

McDermott, Gerald R. *One Holy and Happy Society: The Public Theology of Jonathan Edwards.* University Park: Pennsylvania State University Press, 1992.

Story, Ronald. *Jonathan Edwards and the Gospel of Love.* Amherst: University of Massachusetts Press, 2012.

Other Short Collections of Edwards's Writings

Kimnach, Wilson H., Kenneth P. Minkema, and Douglas A. Sweeney, eds. *The Sermons of Jonathan Edwards: A Reader.* New Haven: Yale University Press, 1999.

Minkema, Kenneth P., John E. Smith, and Harry S. Stout, eds. *A Jonathan Edwards Reader.* New Haven: Yale University Press, 1995.

Biographies

Dods, Elisabeth. *Marriage to a Difficult Man: The Uncommon Union of Jonathan and Sarah Edwards.* Laurel, Miss.: Audubon Press, 2005.

Gura, Philip F. *Jonathan Edwards: America's Evangelical.* New York: Hill and Wang, 2005.

Marsden, George M. *Jonathan Edwards: A Life.* New Haven: Yale University Press, 2003.

Marsden, George M. *A Short Life of Jonathan Edwards.* Grand Rapids, Mich.: Eerdmans, 2008.

Miller, Perry. *Jonathan Edwards.* 1949. Reprint, Lincoln, Neb.: Bison Books, 2005.

Tracy, Patricia. *Jonathan Edwards, Pastor.* New York: Hill and Wang, 1980.

Winslow, Ola Elizabeth. *Jonathan Edwards, 1703–1758.* New York: Macmillan, 1941.

Surveys of Edwards's Thought

Cherry, Conrad. *The Theology of Jonathan Edwards: A Reappraisal.* Bloomington: Indiana University Press, 1966.

McClymond, Michael J., and Gerald R. McDermott. *The Theology of Jonathan Edwards.* New York: Oxford University Press, 2012.

Smith, John E. *Jonathan Edwards: Puritan, Preacher, Philosopher.* Notre Dame, Ind.: University of Notre Dame Press, 1992.

Particular Themes in Edwards's Thought

Bezzant, Rhys S. *Jonathan Edwards and the Church.* New York: Oxford University Press, 2014.

Brown, Robert E. *Jonathan Edwards and the Bible.* Bloomington: Indiana University Press, 2002.

Danaher, William J., Jr. *The Trinitarian Ethics of Jonathan Edwards.* Louisville, Ky.: Westminster John Knox Press, 2004.

Fiering, Norman. *Jonathan Edwards: Moral Thought and Its British Context.* Chapel Hill: University of North Carolina Press, 1981.

McDermott, Gerald R. *Jonathan Edwards Confronts the Gods: Christian Theology, Enlightenment Religion, and Non-Christian Faiths.* New York: Oxford University Press, 2000.

McDermott, Gerald R. *Seeing God: Jonathan Edwards and Spiritual Discernment.* Vancouver: Regent College Publishing, 1995.

Pauw, Amy Plantinga. *The Supreme Harmony of All: The Trinitarian Theology of Jonathan Edwards.* Grand Rapids, Mich.: Eerdmans, 2002.

Wilson, Stephen A. *Virtue Reformed: Rereading Jonathan Edwards's Ethics.* Leiden: Brill, 2005.

Zakai, Avihu. *Jonathan Edwards's Philosophy of History: The Reenchantment of the World in the Age of Enlightenment.* Princeton: Princeton University Press, 2003.

Zakai, Avihu. *Jonathan Edwards's Philosophy of Nature: The Reenchantment of the World in an Age of Scientific Reasoning.* New York: T&T International, 2010.

Collections of Scholarly Articles

Hart, D. G., Sean Michael Lucas, and Stephen J. Nichols, eds. *The Legacy of Jonathan Edwards: American Religion and the Evangelical Tradition.* Grand Rapids, Mich.: Baker, 2003.

Hatch, Nathan O., and Harry S. Stout, eds. *Jonathan Edwards and the American Experience.* New York: Oxford University Press, 1988.

Kling, David W., and Douglas A. Sweeney, eds. *Jonathan Edwards at Home and Abroad: Historical Memories, Cultural Movements, Global Horizons.* Columbia: University of South Carolina Press, 2003.

Lee, Sang Hyun, and Alan Guelzo, eds. *Edwards in Our Time: Jonathan Edwards and the Shaping of American Religion.* Grand Rapids, Mich.: Eerdmans, 2000.

Oberg, Barbara O., and Harry S. Stout, eds. *Benjamin Franklin, Jonathan Edwards, and the Representation of American Culture.* New York: Oxford University Press, 1993.

Schweitzer, Don, ed. *Jonathan Edwards as Contemporary: Essays in Honor of Sang Hyun Lee.* New York: Peter Lang, 2010.

Stein, Stephen J., ed. *The Cambridge Companion to Jonathan Edwards.* Cambridge: Cambridge University Press, 2006.

Northampton and the Connecticut Valley

Buckley, Kerry, ed. *A Place Called Paradise: Culture and Community in Northampton, Massachusetts, 1651–2004.* Northampton and Amherst: Historic Northampton in association with University of Massachusetts Press, 2004.

Clark, Christopher. *The Roots of Rural Capitalism: Western Massachusetts, 1780–1860*. Ithaca, N.Y.: Cornell University Press, 1990.

Lucas, Paul. *Valley of Discord: Church and Society along the Connecticut River, 1636–1725*. Hanover, N.H.: University Press of New England, 1976.

Nobles, Gregory H. *Divisions throughout the Whole: Politics and Society in Hampshire County, Massachusetts, 1740–1775*. New York: Cambridge University Press, 1983.

Romer, Robert. *Slavery in the Connecticut Valley of Massachusetts*. Amherst, Mass.: Levellers Press, 2009.

The Historical Context of Edwards's Life and Thought

Axtell, James. *The Invasion Within: The Contest of Cultures in Colonial North America*. New York: Oxford University Press, 1985.

Beeman, Richard. *The Varieties of Political Experience in Eighteenth Century America*. Philadelphia: University of Pennsylvania Press, 2004.

Kidd, Thomas. *The Great Awakening: The Roots of Evangelical Christianity in Colonial America*. New Haven: Yale University Press, 2007.

Knight, Janice. *Orthodoxies in Massachusetts: Rereading American Puritanism*. Cambridge: Harvard University Press, 1994.

Peterson, Mark. *The Price of Redemption: The Spiritual Economy of Puritan New England*. Stanford: Stanford University Press, 1997.

Stout, Harry. *The New England Soul: Preaching and Religious Culture in Colonial New England*. New York: Oxford University Press, 1986.

Todd, Margo. *Christian Humanism and the Puritan Social Order*. Cambridge: Cambridge University Press, 1987.

Valeri, Mark. *Heavenly Merchandize: How Religion Shaped Commerce in Puritan America*. Princeton: Princeton University Press, 2010.

Warch, Richard. *School of the Prophets: Yale College, 1701–1740*. New Haven: Yale University Press, 1973.

The Yale Edition of *The Works of Jonathan Edwards*

The bulk of Edwards's writings are available in twenty-six printed volumes published by Yale University Press. Each volume has a lengthy scholarly introduction. A seventy-three-volume digitized edition of Edwards's writings, also published by Yale University Press, is available online through the Jonathan Edwards Center at Yale. The following volumes of the printed Yale edition are particularly relevant to Edwards's social ministry and vision:

Vol. 2. *Religious Affections,* ed. John E. Smith.
Vol. 4. *The Great Awakening,* ed. C. C. Goen.
    A Faithful Narrative
    The Distinguishing Marks
    Some Thoughts Concerning the Revival
    Preface to True Religion by Joseph Bellamy
Vol. 5. *Apocalyptic Writings,* ed. Stephen J. Stein.
    Notes on the Apocalypse
    An Humble Attempt

Vol. 8. *Ethical Writings*, ed. Paul Ramsey.
   Charity and Its Fruits
   Concerning the End for Which God Created the World
   The Nature of True Virtue
Vol. 9. *A History of the Work of Redemption*, ed. John F. Wilson.
Vol. 10. *Sermons and Discourses, 1720–1723*, ed. Wilson H. Kimnach.
Vol. 12. *Ecclesiastical Writings*, ed. David D. Hall.
   A Letter to the Author of an Answer to the Hampshire Narrative
   An Humble Inquiry
   Misrepresentations Corrected
   Narrative of Communion Controversy
Vol. 13. *The "Miscellanies," a–500*, ed. Thomas A. Schafer.
Vol. 14. *Sermons and Discourses, 1723–1729*, ed. Kenneth P. Minkema.
Vol. 17. *Sermons and Discourses, 1730–1733*, ed. Mark Valeri.
Vol. 18. *The "Miscellanies," 501–832*, ed. Ava Chamberlin.
Vol. 19. *Sermons and Discourses, 1734–1738*, ed. M. X. Lesser.
Vol. 20. *The "Miscellanies," 833–1152*, ed. Amy Plantinga Pauw.
Vol. 22. *Sermons and Discourses, 1739–1742*, ed. Harry S. Stout and Nathan O. Hatch.
Vol. 23. *The "Miscellanies," 1153–1360*, ed. Douglas A. Sweeney.
Vol. 25. *Sermons and Discourses, 1743–1758*, ed. Wilson H. Kimnach.
Vol. 26. *Catalogue of Reading*, ed. Peter J. Theusen.
   Catalogue of Reading
   Account Book

INDEX

GERALD MCDERMOTT is the Jordan-Trexler Professor of Religion at Roanoke College; Research Associate at the Jonathan Edwards Centre Africa, University of the Free State, South Africa; and Distinguished Senior Fellow, Baylor Institute for Studies of Religion. He is the author or coauthor of fifteen books, including five other books on Jonathan Edwards. His coauthored *Theology of Jonathan Edwards* (Oxford University Press) won *Christianity Today*'s Book Award in Theology/Ethics for 2103. He and his wife, Jean, have three grown sons and eight grandchildren.

RONALD STORY is Professor of History Emeritus at the University of Massachusetts Amherst. He has published extensively in U.S. political, cultural, and social history and the history of the Second World War. Among his eight books is, most recently, *Jonathan Edwards and the Gospel of Love* (University of Massachusetts Press). He was for many years a deacon in the First Churches of Northampton, which stands where Jonathan Edwards once preached. He lives in South Deerfield, not far from the Great Deerfield Indian Raid of Edwards's early years.